Л030696Z

Maisie Parrish's

Cakes with Character

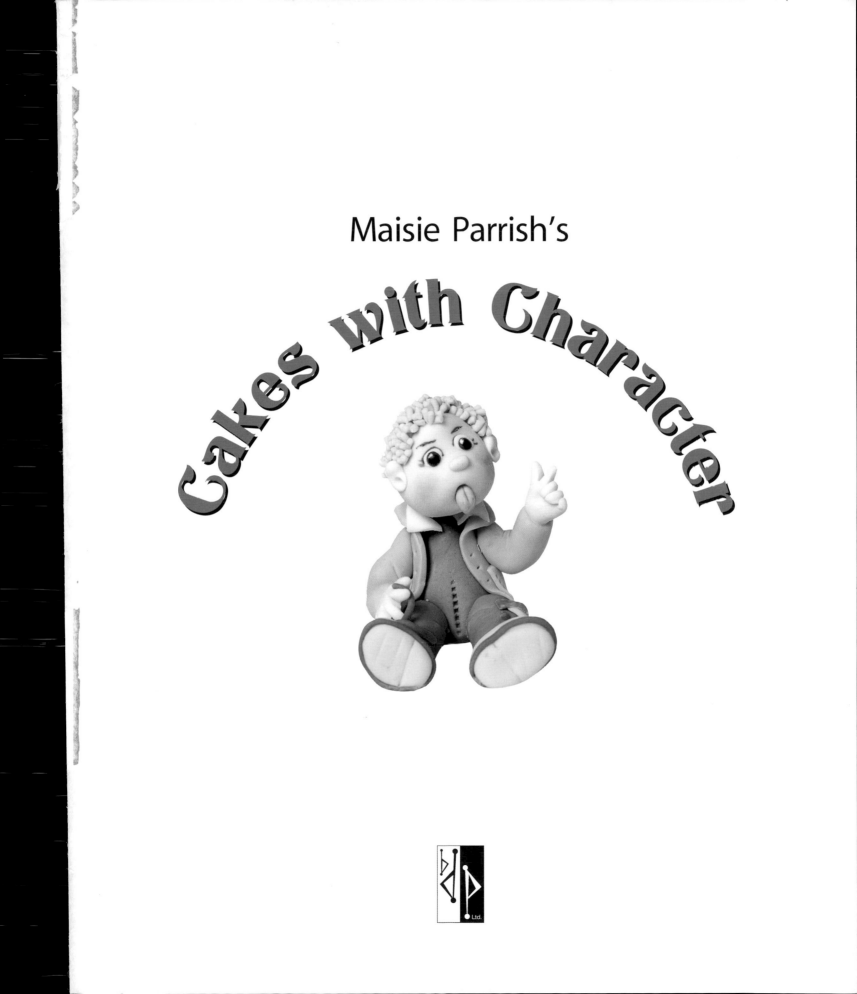

Ltd.

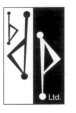

Dedicated to Mum and Dad – I miss you.

First published in March 2006 by B. Dutton Publishing Limited, The Grange, Hones Yard, Farnham, Surrey, GU9 8BB.

Reprinted in Sepember 2010

Copyright: Maisie Parrish 2006

ISBN-10: 1-905113-03-X

ISBN-13: 978-1-905113-03-3

All rights reserved.

No part of this publication may be reproduced, stored in a retrieval system or transmitted in any form or by means electronic, mechanical, photocopying, recording, or otherwise, without prior written permission of the copyright owner. A catalogue record of this book is available from the British Library.

Maisie Parrish has asserted her right under the Copyright, Designs and Patents Act, 1988, to be identified as the author of this work.

Publisher: Beverley Dutton

Editor: Jenny Stewart

Designer: Sarah Richardson

Editorial Assistant: Clare Porter

Design Assistant: Zena Manicom

Photography: Alister Thorpe

Printed in China

Acknowledgements

I would like to acknowledge the hard work and dedication of everyone in B. Dutton Publishing, particularly Jenny and Sarah for putting this book together so beautifully, and also Alister for his wonderful photography; my especial thanks go to Beverley.

The Author and Publisher have made every effort to ensure that the contents of this book, if followed carefully, will not cause harm or injury or pose any danger. Please note that some non-edible items such as wires, plastic dowelling rods and flower stamens have been used in the cakes in this book. All such non-edible items must be removed before the cake is eaten. Similarly, any non food-grade equipment and substances such as non-toxic glue must not come into contact with any cake or cake covering that is to be eaten. Neither the Author nor the Publisher can be held responsible for errors or omissions and cannot accept liability for injury, damage or loss to persons or property however it may arise as a result of acting upon guidelines and information printed in this book.

Foreword

Photograph: Steve Lee Studios

When you make a cake, everything has to be perfect – not only the ingredients, but also the method and cooking time, otherwise it simply will not work. Once the cake is made, decorating it with fun, amusing characters to tell a story is another challenge entirely, requiring great skill, care, patience and attention to detail. Speaking with my chef's hat on, whilst bread, puddings, ice creams, and a multitude of other sweet treats are not a problem, I can quite honestly say that baking is not usually a strong point with any chef.

This is why I have the utmost respect for great cake bakers and sugarcrafters like Maisie, and the reason why I, and many other people, have shelves full of good cake making books.

Cakes with Character is an amazing book packed with not only great ideas, but also with simple, easy-to-follow instructions and guidance. The photographs are stunning, and you can see the real quality of her work. I especially love *Kitchen Capers*, Maisie's tribute to TV chefs!

This book is a must not only for the serious cake maker, but also for the enthusiastic amateur and first timers. I urge you all to get stuck into these great ideas and marvel at the results… I can promise you will not be disappointed!

Introduction

Cakes with Character is a collection of fun and adventurous projects which bring new life to figure modelling in sugar. Modelling is a real art form, as it requires a combination of both skill and interpretation. It is an exciting experience to create and develop unique characters of your own, each one with its own shape, personality and features.

As you practise figure modelling and become more accomplished, you can really bring your characters to life. First of all you need to develop the character by giving the body movement and shaping the hands to create expressions; the posture and position of the head will then add to each character's personality. The animated gestures and expressions you create provide dialogue without words, so every cake tells a story.

Before you embark on a project, study your own face in the mirror, and watch other people as their faces go through different emotions. By mimicking many different expressions in your sugar characters, you can be sure to keep your work interesting and amusing.

I hope this collection of cakes will inspire you to be creative and have fun whilst you craft your very own characters in sugar. With so much to discover, I wish you success and lots of enjoyment.

Best wishes,

Maisie

Contents

Tools and Equipment

In addition to the basic tools required for covering a cake, you will find that there are many products on the market designed for sugar modelling. The following items are used for most, if not all, the projects in the book, so are worth investing in. Other specialist equipment is given at the beginning of each project.

Essential items:

Blossom plunger cutters: set of 3

Cake smoother with handle

Circle cutter set: small (CT)

Cocktail sticks/CelStick (CC)

Craft knife

Cutting wheels: plain and patterned (PME)

High quality paintbrushes (SK)

Marzipan knife (SK)

Modelling tools (SK)

Palette knife

Polythene (non-stick) board

Polythene rolling pins: large and small

Raw spaghetti

Rectangular cutter set: small (CT)

Spacers and Sizing Cutters set (SK)

Sugar Dough Press (SK)

TIP When you are using cutters, a little fat smeared on the inside edge of the cutter will help the paste to slide off smoothly.

Keep all your tools and equipment clean and free from grease. All modelling tools, boards, cutters, etc. should be washed in warm, soapy water and kept together (a pencil case is ideal). All edible materials should be stored according to the manufacturers' instructions.

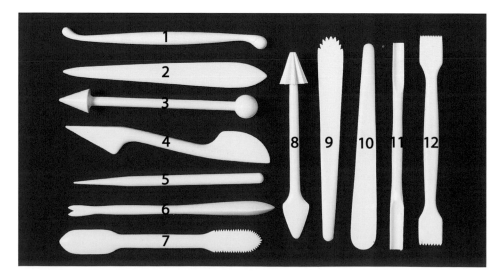

Modelling Tools (SK)

Tool	Uses
1	Both ends can be used for making indentations (such as eyes and mouth) and to thin petals and leaves.
2	A tool useful for smoothing joins and marking veins on leaves.
3	The rounded end is useful for moulding a hollow shape from a ball of paste; the pointed end is useful for hollowing out cones.
4	A cutting tool for making clean straight cuts and markings.
5	Both ends can be used for making eye sockets, nostrils and buttons; the pointed end can be used to frill paste.
6	Use this tool to indent a shell pattern onto a cake or board for a quick finish; use the narrow end to smooth over paste when using moulds.
7	The serrated end can be used to make stitch marks on curved or flat shapes and to texture clothing; the smooth end is useful for blending joins.
8	The pointed, star-shaped end can be used to indent the top of fruit, make buttons and create a decorative pattern; the flat end can create parallel straight lines and is useful for trellis work.
9	The serrated end can be used for making rough textures for feathers, grass or wood; the rounded end creates a smooth indentation or channel.
10	A blunt tool used to hollow out rounded shapes, make arches, and for smoothing paste.
11	An invaluable tool for marking smiles, eyes and eyebrows on faces; also useful for fish scales.
12	A double-ended serrated tool used for making deep or fine stitch marks, useful when making teddy bears and clothing.

Basic Techniques

If you are new to cake decorating, it is worth mastering these basic techniques as you will use them every time you decorate a cake.

Covering a Cake Drum (Board)

All of the projects in this book will require a cake and cake drum (board) to be covered (iced). There are two ways in which a cake board can be covered, so choose whichever you prefer.

Method 1

1. Begin with a clean work surface – a large, non-stick polythene board is ideal. Rub a little white vegetable fat over the surface or dust with icing sugar (in a shaker).

2. Knead the sugarpaste with a little white vegetable fat on your hands until it is smooth and pliable. Form it into a smooth, oval ball, then roll it out using a large polythene rolling pin, keeping in mind the shape you are trying to achieve.

3. Hold the cake drum over the paste to see if it is large enough; if not, continue to roll out the paste.

4. Brush the surface of the cake drum with a little cooled, boiled water. This will help the paste to stick, so it is important that the entire surface is moist.

5. Lift the edge of the sugarpaste over the rolling pin, pick up the paste and lay it over the cake drum.

Working with Sugar Dough

Sugar Dough is an edible medium which is ideal for modelling and can also be used as a cake covering. It is available in the following ready-made colours:

Black

Blue

Brown

Flesh

Golden Bear Brown

Green

Maroon

Orange

Peach

Red

Violet

White

Yellow

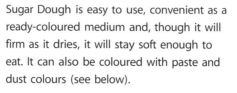

Sugar Dough is easy to use, convenient as a ready-coloured medium and, though it will firm as it dries, it will stay soft enough to eat. It can also be coloured with paste and dust colours (see below).

Sugar Dough will fulfil most tasks very well without the need to add anything to it. However, there are two instances where you may wish to do so:

• When extruding paste through a Sugar Dough Press or sugar shaper, the paste must be soft in consistency. Knead a little white vegetable fat into the paste before pushing it through the press.

• If you are making something that is a supportive piece and therefore requires a little bit of extra strength, add a little gum tragacanth to the paste.

Storing Sugar Dough

Once you have opened a packet of Sugar Dough, it is important to keep any remaining paste airtight. Rather than leaving it in the opened packet where it will dry out, rub a little white vegetable fat over your hands and knead the paste until it is soft and pliable. Roll it into a thick sausage shape and wrap it up tightly in a couple of layers of clingfilm, then put this into a resealable food-grade plastic bag and roll up tightly to exclude any air. Sugar Dough can be frozen in this way, but must be thoroughly defrosted before use. Alternatively, you can keep the wrapped paste in an airtight food

container at room temperature, so the paste will keep and be ready for use whenever you need it. If the Sugar Dough feels a little stiff when you take it out, rub a little white vegetable fat over your hands and knead it well before use.

> **TIP** When using Sugar Dough, always make sure it is smooth and supple before you begin to model shapes or roll out. This can be achieved by kneading the paste for a few minutes.

Colouring Sugar Dough

Although Sugar Dough is available in a range of ready-to-use colours, you can add food colour to it to create an even wider range of colours. If you have a selection of paste colours to hand, this can also be useful if only a tiny amount of Sugar Dough is required for a project as you can colour the paste rather than opening a new pack. Food colours are available in three forms: paste, liquid and dust (powder), which can be used to create different effects.

Paste Colours

To colour Sugar Dough and other roll-out pastes such as sugarpaste, knead in a little SK Paste Food Colour. Add the paste colour a little at a time to the Sugar Dough using a cocktail stick, then knead well until the colour is even. It is worth remembering that it is easier to make the colour more intense than it is to make it paler. (If you find that you have added too much colour, knead some White Sugar Dough to the coloured paste.) You will find that the paste colour can stain your hands, so you may wish to wear a pair of food-grade plastic gloves when colouring the Sugar Dough.

Paste food colours are also a good medium for painting onto Sugar Dough. Simply dilute the paste colour with cooled, boiled water and paint onto the sugar. For a translucent effect, more water can be added, but do not add too much moisture to the surface of the Sugar Dough otherwise it will start to dissolve.

Dust Colours

SK Dust Food Colours are easy to work with and lend themselves brilliantly to shading and adding highlights to Sugar Dough. They are also ideal for painting sugar, particularly when you want it to dry quickly: add clear alcohol (for example gin or vodka) to the dust and mix to a smooth consistency. When you are working on a

particular project, it is advisable to have a small paint palette on which to mix the colours. Although the alcohol will evaporate fairly rapidly, there is no need to wash the leftover dust colour away before finishing the project as the addition of more alcohol will bring it back to painting consistency again the next time you need it.

In addition to the regular colour ranges, lustrous, pastel, iridescent, glitter and sparkle-effect edible dusts are available, giving you a great deal of scope when decorating and colouring your sugar work.

Liquid Colours

If you are surface-painting Sugar Dough, SK Liquid Food Colours can be used instead of diluted paste colours. For example, where a pattern is required on an item of clothing, the liquid colour can simply be painted onto the sugar.

How to Measure Colours

If you are making a particular shade of paste, you may wish to record how much colour you have used so that the same colour can be made again. Always weigh

the paste in the first instance, then measure the colour you are adding. If you are using liquid food colour, simply record the number of drops used. Recording the amount of paste or dust colour used is more difficult, so always keep a small swatch of the coloured paste for comparison. A set of measuring spoons is available which record a 'smidgen', a 'pinch' or a 'dash' (Lakeland Plastics), but if you can't get hold of these, try putting a certain amount on the end of a cocktail stick or spoon and record how many times colour must be added to obtain the required shade. As long as you weigh the Sugar Dough in the first instance, you can work from there. Always write down your colouring methods so that you can refer to them later.

Marbling

Sugar Dough in different colours can be marbled together to create a range of effects: I use marbling for floors, marble pedestals, water, rocks and wood, for example. To marble two or more colours, roll a long sausage of each colour, then twist them together and roll into one big sausage. Roll this up and then form into a ball. Repeat the process until the desired effect is achieved, taking care not to blend the colours too much.

Figure Modelling

The figures in this book are all made from basic shapes. Once you have mastered the simple techniques of creating the three basic forms – a ball, cone and sausage – modelling any figure is straightforward.

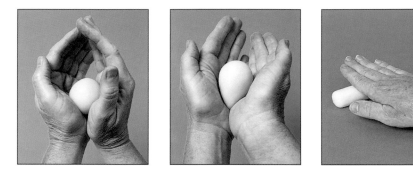

Proportions

I have used the SK Spacers and Sizing Cutters set throughout the book to ensure the figures are correctly proportioned. Simply roll out the Sugar Dough in the appropriate colour between the two spacers (grooves upwards unless otherwise specified). When the surface is smooth and even, the rolling pin will touch the top of the spacers, giving the depth of paste required. Use one of the cutters – no. 1 (3cm) to no. 4 (6cm) – to cut out the quantity of paste required and proceed to model the shape required.

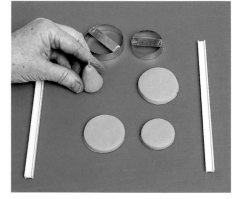

The spacers and sizing cutters can be used to make people, animals and teddy bears using the relevant cutters.

How to Make a Teddy Bear

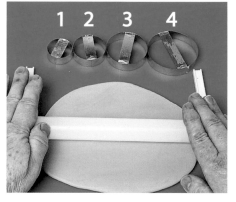

1. Roll out a ball of paste between the two spacers using a non-stick rolling pin.

2. Cut out four circles using cutter no. 3 and one using no. 2. Form one of the larger circles into a cone for the body and insert a length of spaghetti into the top.

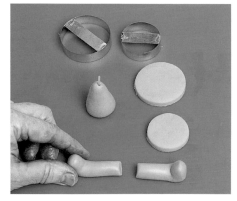

3. To make the legs, roll a sausage from a no. 3 circle, turn up the ends and cut in half.

4. Secure the legs to the body. Add a tummy button and stitch marks down the centre.

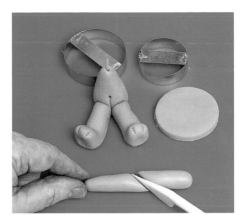

5. Roll the no. 2 circle into a sausage and make a diagonal cut in the centre for the arms.

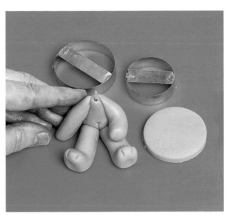

6. Secure the arms to the top of the body and bend into position.

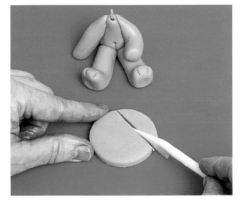

7. Take the last no. 3 circle and cut off a section at the top.

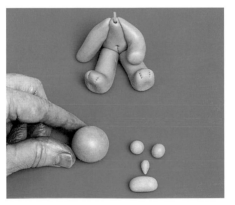

8. Roll the larger portion into a smooth ball for the head and make the ears, snout and nose from the smaller piece.

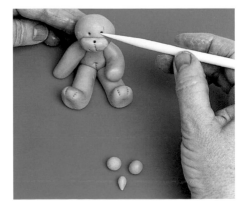

9. Push the head over the spaghetti at the neck. Use a no. 3 modelling tool to mark the eyes, nose and paws.

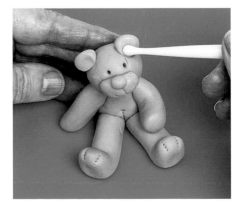

10. Add the nose and ears. Push the ears in place with a no. 1 tool.

Body Shapes and Heads

The head and body of a figure can be made in a number of different ways, depending on how the figure is positioned and how it is to be dressed. There are seven basic shapes (below and overleaf) which show how to make the body and head for different purposes.

A. The head and neck are modelled in one piece to correspond with body B.

B. This is a cone-shaped body without a neck and would be used when the body is to be dressed in a different colour from the head.

C. A round head without a neck is used when the figure has an open neckline and is paired with body D.

D. An inverted cone-shaped body with the neck pulled out at the top is used to create an open neckline.

E. A cone-shaped body with the lower half cut off is used then a figure is

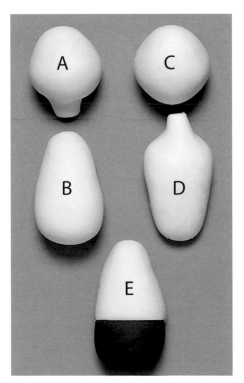

wearing trousers. A second cone is made in the colour of the trousers with the top cut off. Secure the two together to achieve the cone shape.

F. If you are going to cover the top of the body with a loose garment of a different colour, make this body and dress as required.

G. This body is made as in the same way as body F but the top half is cut off and made in another colour. It is a useful shape if you want to arrange the figure in a kneeling position.

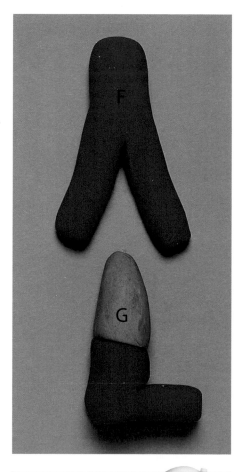

TIP Model each figure on a small cake card so that you can move it around without having to handle it.

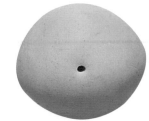

Making a Basic Face

1. Roll a smooth ball of Sugar Dough and make a small hole in the centre of the face for the nose. Make a small cone shape for the nose and glue into the hole.

2. Roll two small teardrop shapes for the ears and attach to the sides of the head in line with the nose. Use the end of a paintbrush to secure and indent the ears.

3. Mark two holes for the eyes with tool no. 1. The eyes should be just above and either side of the nose in a triangle shape. Fill the eyes with small balls of Sugar Dough.

4. Make a smile with tool no. 11, or indent with the edge of a small circle cutter if you require a bigger smile.

5. Outline the eyebrows with diluted paste food colour. Paint the mouth with pink or red paste food colour, then water some down further to blush the cheeks. Alternatively, use pink lustre dust applied with a dry brush.

6. Finally, extrude paste through a Sugar Dough Press for the hair and secure to the head with edible glue.

Creating Expressions

TIP When working on the head for a figure, place it in a curved former rather than on a flat surface to help it keep its shape.

Arms and Hands

When making arms for a figure, they should start right at the top of the shoulder and come to about halfway down the thigh. Always ensure the arms are in the correct proportion before finishing off the detail. The easiest way to ensure they are the same length is to roll out one sausage of paste, measure it and make a diagonal cut in the centre.

If the figure is wearing long sleeves, make the arms and hands separately and secure the hands in place with a piece of raw spaghetti. If the figure has bare arms, you will need to model the arms and hands together, which takes a little more practice. Narrow the paste at the wrist and elbow and finish the hand in the usual way.

TIP I always use edible glue to secure the modelled parts. Apply with a fine brush, taking care not to put too much on to your work, as this will cause the pieces to slip. Where an extra strong sugar glue is required, mix pastillage powder with edible glue (or clear alcohol for a quick-drying glue) to a paste.

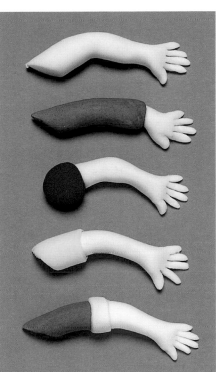

TIP Where pieces need extra support, raw spaghetti can be inserted into the Sugar Dough to keep the pieces together. As this is edible, it is perfectly safe to use but must be removed before the decorations are eaten.

Legs and Feet

When you are making the legs, always remember that they should start at the hip, rather than at the top of the thigh. In terms of proportion, the legs should be about the same length as the body and should be slightly thicker for male figures than for female.

To make the legs and feet in one, roll out a long sausage of paste and cut in the centre. Make a steep diagonal cut at the top of each leg so that it fits at the hip. Flatten a section at the bottom of each leg for the foot, thin the lower half of the leg, then shape the knee and ankle by rolling with your little finger. Shape the foot and mark the toes with the back of a knife. (There is no need to make feet if the figure is wearing shoes.)

If the figure is wearing trousers, simply make the legs in the same colour as the trouser material.

15

Materials

20.5cm (8") square cake

1.4kg (3lb 1oz) white sugarpaste

SK Sugar Dough: 80g ($2^3/_4$oz) Black, 70g ($2^1/_2$oz) Brown, 50g ($1/_4$oz) Flesh, 180g ($6^1/_4$oz) Golden Bear Brown, 100g ($3^1/_2$oz) Green, 20g ($1^3/_4$oz) Red and 300g ($10^1/_2$oz) White

SK Paste Food Colours: Chestnut, Leaf Green and Sunflower

SK Dust Food Colours: Bulrush and Leaf Green

SK Pastel Dust Colour: Pastel Pink

SK Edible Glue

Raw spaghetti

White vegetable fat

❀

Equipment

30.5cm (12") square cake drum

Non-stick board and rolling pin

SK Modelling Tools

SK Spacers and Sizing Cutters

SK Sugar Dough Press

SK Paintbrush: no. 2

Bark and brick impression mats (FMM)

Circle cutters: small (CT)

Rectangular cutters (CT)

Gymkhana

It can be such fun to ride a pony but sometimes they just won't jump! Horse riders of all ages will love this equestrian cake.

Covering the Cake and Board

Colour the sugarpaste with Leaf Green Paste Food Colour. Use half the paste to cover the board and the other half to cover the cake. Place the cake centrally on the board and allow to firm.

Fence

1. Roll out 80g of White Sugar Dough between two spacers to create an even thickness. Cut a strip measuring 1cm x 10cm and cut this in half. Push a length of dry spaghetti through the centre, leaving a little showing at the base. Set aside to firm.

2. To make the cross supports, cut a strip measuring 1cm x 8cm. Cut this strip in half, and then cut one piece in half again. Repeat for the second cross section. Glue the two short pieces to the longer one to make a cross.

3. Make the poles by rolling a piece of White Sugar Dough into a sausage shape measuring 18cm long. Carefully push a piece of raw spaghetti through the centre and re-roll to an even thickness. Trim the ends neatly. Repeat to make a second pole. Roll out some Black Sugar Dough thinly and cut out three rectangles to wrap around the poles. Space them evenly and glue into position.

4. Lay the upright posts flat on the work surface and lay the black and white poles over the top. Secure the poles to the posts using edible glue. Add the supports and set aside to dry.

5. Apply some glue to the base of the posts and attach them to the centre of the cross pieces. The spaghetti at the base of the upright post should give support. Prop up the completed fence so that it dries upright before securing to the cake.

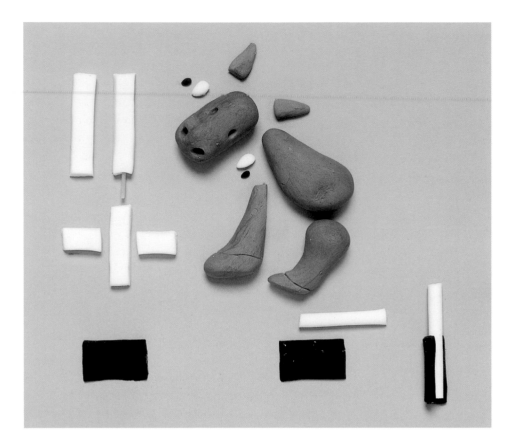

leaf shapes and place these on top of the strap. Roll a small round ball for the saddle, flatten with your finger and lift up at the back. Glue the saddle over the leaf shapes. Make the stirrups by rolling a thin strip of grey paste, make a loop and adjust the length as required.

> **TIP** Keep any leftover grey Sugar Dough to make some of the small items on the cake later.

7. To make the horse's mane and tail, soften 35g of White Sugar Dough with a little white vegetable fat. Extrude the paste through the Sugar Dough Press to make the mane and tail, cut to length and secure to the horse with edible glue.

Girl Rider

1. To make the jodhpurs, add 5g of White Sugar Dough to 10g of Golden Bear Brown. Roll the paste into an oval shape and slightly flatten with your hand. Using tool no. 4, divide the paste to make the legs, keeping the top part joined. Roll the legs between your fingers to make the edges smooth and rounded and position them astride the horse. Make two small, black boots, add a small sole made from Golden Bear Brown Sugar Dough and mark the heel using tool no. 4.

2. Mix together equal amounts of Red and Yellow Sugar Dough and add a little Flesh to make the colour for the girl's top. Roll 5g into a cone shape for the body, make a straight cut at the bottom and secure to the trousers. Roll another 5g into a sausage shape for the arms, make a diagonal cut in the centre and trim to size. Secure to the top of the body in an outstretched position. Before adding the hands, place a thin strip from the bridle over the top of the mane and around to

Grey Pony

1. Add 15g of Black Sugar Dough to 100g of White Sugar Dough to make a grey shade. Roll 35g of this paste into a cone and push a piece of raw spaghetti down through the centre, leaving 3cm showing at the top.

2. Divide 25g of the grey paste in half and roll each piece into a fat cone shape for the back legs. Flatten at the end and shape the hoof, then mark with tool no. 4.

3. For the front legs, divide 25g of the grey paste in half and roll each piece into a sausage shape. Shape a hoof and mark as before. Secure to the front of the body using edible glue.

4. For the head, roll 20g of paste into an oval shape. Narrow slightly in the centre, and flatten the front. Mark the nostrils by pushing the end of a paintbrush into the front. Mark the smile with a small, round cutter and insert a small strip of white for the teeth. Mark the eyes with the end of a paintbrush on either side of the head. Add some glue to the top of the body and push the head over the spaghetti.

5. Make two small cone shapes and flatten them for the ears. Attach them to each side of the head. Add a touch of edible glue to the eye sockets and insert a small ball of White Sugar Dough. Add a small ball of Black Sugar Dough for the pupil.

6. To make the saddle, harness and bridle you will require 25g of Golden Bear Brown Sugar Dough. Make the bridle by rolling out and cutting a thin strip to go across the nose, then attach two more strips to the side of the face. Do not add the reins at this stage. To make the saddle strap, roll out a strip measuring 9cm and place this around the horse. Cut out two

the same cutter to create the peak of the hat. Apply some glue to the edge of the peak and secure to the head.

5. Extrude a few strands of Brown Sugar Dough through the Sugar Dough Press and twist two together to make curls. Arrange them around the edge of the cap.

Brown Horse

1. To make the body, roll 35g of Brown Sugar Dough into a smooth cone shape and turn up the end for the neck. Push a piece of raw spaghetti down through the centre of the neck, leaving 3cm showing at the top.

2. Make four short legs from approximately 30g of Brown Sugar Dough. Roll each piece into a cone shape, flatten at the end and add a black hoof. Mark around the hoof using tool no. 4. Push a small piece of dry spaghetti down through the centre of each leg, leaving 3cm showing at the top. Set the legs aside to dry before attaching to the body with edible glue.

3. Make the head as previously described but omit the teeth. Soften 30g of Black Sugar Dough with white vegetable fat and extrude through the Sugar Dough Press as before to make the horse's mane and tail.

the other side. Then add a small ball for each hand, just marking the thumb.

3. Push a small piece of raw spaghetti down through the top of the body. Make the head by rolling 5g of Flesh Sugar Dough into a ball. Mark the centre of the face using tool no. 5. Add a tiny cone shape for the nose, and then mark the eyes in the same way, just above and either side of the nose. Fill with small balls of Black or Brown Sugar Dough. Mark the mouth with

the end of a paintbrush to give the face a surprised look. Add two small teardrop shapes for the ears and attach to each side of the head. Blush the cheeks with Pastel Pink Dust Food Colour.

4. To make the riding hat, roll 5g of Blue Sugar Dough into a ball for the crown, make a straight cut at the base and glue to the head. Roll out a little more Blue Sugar Dough and cut out a 2.5cm circle, then remove two thirds of the circle with

Boy Rider

1. To make the lower body, roll 10g of White Sugar Dough into a ball, make a straight cut at the waist and glue the rounded end to the saddle. Push a piece of raw spaghetti down through the centre, leaving 3cm showing at the top.

2. Roll 5g of White Sugar Dough into a sausage shape for the legs and make a diagonal cut in the centre. Bend at the knee and push a tiny piece of dry spaghetti into the end of the legs where the feet will be. Make two small boots as before and secure them to the legs. Secure the completed legs to the body and the side of the horse. Roll a grey strip for the stirrup and glue this around the front of the boot.

3. Complete the upper body, arms, hands and head as before, but this time mark a small smile on the face. Add the hands after you have put the reins into place.

4. For the hair, add a little Chestnut Paste Food Colour to 15g of Golden Bear Brown Sugar Dough. Soften the paste with a little white vegetable fat and extrude through the Sugar Dough Press. Apply a few strands at a time around the head, starting at the back. Make a riding hat from Black Sugar Dough as previously described and secure onto the head.

Stables

1. Blend 25g of White Sugar Dough with an equal amount of Golden Bear Brown. Roll into a sausage shape and then using a rolling pin, make a shape to fit the bark impression mat. Place the mat on the top of the Sugar Dough, press down firmly and roll over it evenly. Using tool no. 4, trim off any excess paste around the edges. Cut the rectangle in half and then cut out two windows measuring 4cm x 2.5cm using the largest rectangle cutter. Place the two doors in the centre front of the cake side and secure with edible glue. Make a strip measuring 14cm x 1.5cm for the roof and cut diagonally at each end. Set aside.

3. Roll out some Golden Bear Brown Sugar Dough and make the wall using the brick matt impression mat. Trim to size and secure to the cake using edible glue. Secure the roof in place at the top.

4. Roll a small ball of grey Sugar Dough for the large nail on the brickwork to hold some reins. Push a piece of raw spaghetti into the wall and slip the nail over it, adding a little glue to secure it in place. Cut a long strip of Red Sugar Dough for the reins and glue them in place. Make a small horseshoe for the opposite side and mark with tool no. 3.

5. Make two horses' heads from Brown Sugar Dough as previously described. Add a small crescent of White Sugar Dough to the nose of one horse and two small, black squares for the blinkers.

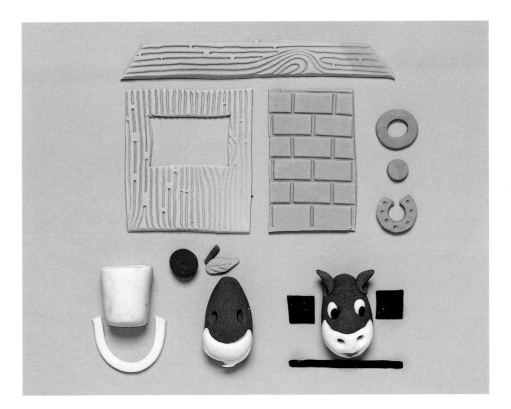

7. To make the hay bale, add a little Sunflower Paste Food Colour to 20g of Flesh Sugar Dough to make a straw colour. Soften the paste with white vegetable fat and extrude several strands through the Sugar Dough Press. Lay them on top of each other in a crisscross fashion.

To Finish

1. Decorate the three remaining sides of the board with clumps of grass. Soften 100g of Green Sugar Dough and fill the Sugar Dough Press, extrude very short strands, then chop them off using too no. 4. They should stay in a clump on the end of the tool. Apply some edible glue to the cake, slide the clump off with a paintbrush and secure in place.

2. Using a dry brush, dust the top of the cake with Bulrush and Leaf Green Dust Food Colours to give the effect of grass. Be careful not to colour the figures on the cake.

6. Make a small bucket from 30g of pale grey Sugar Dough. Start by modelling a cone, then cut off the top and bottom and hollow out the inside using tool no. 3. Add a small strip for the handle and secure by pushing in the tip of tool no. 3. Make a few apples using leftover pieces of Red and Green Sugar Dough, indent the top with tool no. 3 and add a stalk and leaf. Fill the bucket with apples and place one on the board.

Materials

15cm x 20.5cm (6" x 8") and 20.5cm x 25.5cm (8" x 10") oval cakes

1.7kg (3lb 12oz) white sugarpaste

SK Sugar Dough: 110g (3^3/$_4$oz) Black, 15g (^{1}/$_2$oz) Blue, 135g (4^1/$_2$oz) Brown, 145g (5oz) Flesh, 175g (6^1/$_4$oz) Golden Bear Brown, 145g (5oz) Green, 70g (2^1/$_2$oz) Red, 300g (10^1/$_2$oz) White, 45g (1^1/$_2$oz) Yellow

SK Paste Food Colours: Blackberry, Bluebell, Chestnut, Fern, Holly/Ivy and Teddy Bear Brown

SK Dust Food Colours: Bluebell, Cyclamen, Daffodil, Edelweiss, Holly/Ivy and Sunflower

SK Designer Dust Colour: Etruscan Brick

SK Liquid Food Colours: Blackberry, Bulrush, Marigold, Mint and Poinsettia

120g (4^1/$_4$oz) SK Pastillage

SK Edible Glue

Raw spaghetti

White vegetable fat

❁

Equipment

28cm x 33cm (11" x 13") round cake drum

15cm x 20.5cm (6" x 8") oval cake card

Non-stick board and rolling pin

SK Cutter and Spacer Set

SK Modelling Tools

SK Sugar Dough Press

SK Paintbrushes: nos. 0 and 10

Blossom cutter: small

Circle cutters: small (CT)

Square cutters: small (CT)

Brick impression mat (FMM)

Textured rolling pin

Cake dowels

Templates (see page 104)

The Farmer Wants a Wife

Not everyone wants a traditional wedding cake and, if you come from a farming community, this cake is just perfect for the big day. It's full of colour and fun and even the animals are enjoying this very special occasion. It is sure to be a show stopper down on the farm!

Covering the Cakes and Board

1. Colour 480g of white sugarpaste with Teddy Bear Brown Paste Food Colour. Cover the board and set aside to dry.

2. For the large cake, colour 800g of sugarpaste with a hint of Fern Paste Food Colour to make a light green shade. Roll the sugarpaste out and cover the cake. Offset this cake on the covered board, just 1cm from the back edge.

3. Place the small cake onto a cake card of the same size. Colour 200g of white sugarpaste with Bluebell Paste Food Colour and knead this into 400g of white sugarpaste to create a marbled effect. Cover the cake and allow to firm.

4. Dowel the larger cake (see page 9) and place the smaller cake (and cake card) centrally on top.

Hay Cart

I enjoy painting, but if you prefer you can colour the pastillage before you cut it out using SK Paste Food Colours.

1. Roll out 120g of pastillage using the spacers with the grooves facing upwards. Cut out a rectangle measuring 9cm x 6cm for the base. Cut out two strips of the same thickness measuring 1cm x 11cm and cut these in half.

2. Using the spacers with the grooves turned inwards, roll out and cut a 12cm x 1cm strip, then cut this exactly in half for the axles. Push a short piece of raw spaghetti into each end to attach to the wheels later. Roll out some more pastillage to the same thickness. Cut out four 3cm circles for the wheels.

3. Place all the pastillage pieces on a flat, non-stick surface and leave to dry for 12 hours, turning halfway through.

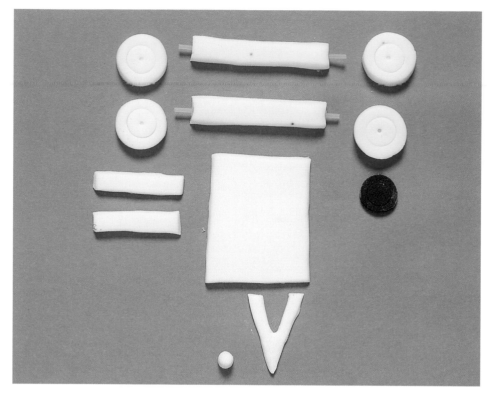

Side Designs

1. To make the hills, divide 75g of Green Sugar Dough into three. Roll out each piece into a rectangle and cut out the hill shapes using the template. Dust patches of Holly/Ivy Dust Food Colour over the surface, then highlight the top of the hills using Sunflower Dust Food Colour. Secure the shapes around the base of the cake, leaving a gap at the back of the cake.

2. Make a fence from 35g of Brown Sugar Dough to fill the gap between the hills. Roll out the paste and cut two 10cm strips, then glue these horizontally along the back of the cake with edible glue. Roll out one long strip of Brown Sugar Dough and cut it into six for the fence posts, marking the wood grain with tool no. 4 or a knife. Add a few tufts of grass, made by extruding short lengths of Green Sugar Dough through a Sugar Dough Press, and some white blossoms (described later when making the pig). Make some more tufts of grass to go around the front of the cake.

Ploughed Field

1. Roll out 25g of Golden Bear Brown Sugar Dough, cut out a strip for the field using the template then adjust the shape to fit onto the board. Use a no. 0 paintbrush and some Bulrush Liquid Food Colour to paint the furrows on the field. Using a clean, dry brush and Etruscan Brick Designer Dust, brush alternate furrows along the field. Apply some edible glue to the cake board and secure the piece into place.

2. Make two small bales of hay by rolling 5g of Golden Bear Brown Sugar Dough into a sausage. Cut off two pieces and paint the rolled swirl on one end of each bale using a no. 0 paintbrush and Bulrush Liquid Food Colour. Stick these onto the ploughed field.

4. To assemble the hay cart, you will need a strong glue to stick the pieces in place; I use pastillage powder mixed with edible glue to form a sticky paste. Place the floor of the cart onto a flat surface and stick the smallest strips across the cart, 1.5cm from each end. Glue the axles on top of these strips and attach the wheels, slipping them over the raw spaghetti at each end. Allow to dry.

5. Paint the assembled cart with a soft brush using Mint and Poinsettia Liquid Food Colours. Begin by painting the underside first and then the top, then set aside once again until dry. (There is no need to paint all over the top of the cart as it will be covered with hay.)

6. Paint the wheels with Blackberry Liquid Food Colour and, when dry, cut out four small hub caps from Red Sugar Dough using a 1.5cm circle cutter and secure in place.

7. To make the hay bales for the cart, mix together 100g of Golden Bear Brown Sugar Dough with 35g of Yellow Sugar Dough. Roll into a thick sausage and cut equally into six portions. Square off each portion with your fingers and prick the end using tool no. 6 or a cocktail stick. Score the top and sides that will be visible with tool, no. 4. Fix the bales to the top of the cart with edible glue and set aside to harden.

3. Make a small fence measuring 6cm from 10g of Brown Sugar Dough. Leave to dry, then glue to the edge of the ploughed field and the side of the cake. Add two tufts of grass to the front of the fence to help anchor the fence in place.

4. Cut out a small tree trunk from 5g of Brown Sugar Dough. Make the leaves from 5g of White Sugar Dough coloured with Holly/Ivy Paste Food Colour. Roll this into a ball and flatten it, then use tool no. 4 to mark the edges. Paint on some apples using Poinsettia Liquid Food Colour. Secure the tree to the side of the cake.

Tractor

1. Roll out 25g of Red Sugar Dough and cut out the shape of the tractor complete with the wheels. Smooth all the edges and outline the door and window using Blackberry Paste Food Colour and a no. 0 paintbrush.

2. Make the thick tyres by rolling out 30g of Black Sugar Dough in-between the spacers. Cut out a 2cm and 1.5cm circle, thinly roll out a little piece of Blue Sugar Dough and cut two smaller circles for the wheel hubs. Stick these to the centre of the wheels then add a small black dot of Blackberry Liquid Food Colour in the centre. Glue the completed wheels to the tractor with edible glue. Make two

small wheel arches from Red Sugar Dough and stick over the tyres.

3. Add a small semi-circle of Golden Bear Brown Sugar Dough for the engine grill and a small cylinder of grey coloured Sugar Dough for the exhaust. Secure the completed tractor to the front of the cake.

Hen House

1. Colour 25g of Golden Bear Brown Sugar Dough with a little Chestnut Paste Food Colour and roll out. Cut out the shape of the hen house and score along the centre of the roof and the top of the walls so that you can fold the paste into position. Cut out the front and back pieces. Cut out two small squares for the windows on the

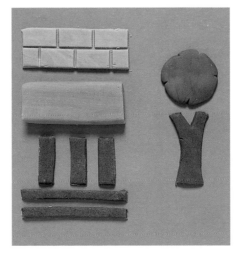

side of the house and a circle for the entrance. Assemble the pieces and then position the house in front of the cake on the board.

2. Make the roof using the template from pale yellow Sugar Dough, score down the middle and mark the tiles with tool no. 4. Secure the roof to the house using edible glue. Make a ramp from a small piece of the Golden Bear Brown Sugar Dough. Leave to dry and then secure to the house.

3. Make a hen by rolling a tiny cone of White Sugar Dough. With the thickest part at the front, add a small yellow beak and a red cone on the head. Position the hen on the roof.

Pig Sty

1. Mix 35g of White Sugar Dough with 15g of Black to make grey. Roll out a sausage shape and flatten. Trim to a 10cm x 2cm rectangle for the wall. Make the bricks by rolling out the remainder of the grey Sugar Dough and place a brick impression mat on top. Gently roll over the mat with a rolling pin to make an imprint on the Sugar Dough. Trim this piece to fit onto the wall then stick to the two pieces together.

2. Make another small fence to go at the back of the sty, adding a little grass to support it as before.

3. Make four piglets using 5g of Flesh Sugar Dough for each. Roll out a small cone shape and stand this up behind the wall. Add two front legs by cutting a tiny sausage shape in half and sticking one piece to either side of the cone. Mark the hoof with tool no. 4 or the back of a knife. Position one piglet so that he is lying down on the floor.

4. Roll a ball for the head and place on the top of the body. Roll a small ball for the snout and mark two nostrils and two holes for the eyes using tool no. 5. To make two small ears, roll a thin cone shape and then flatten it between your finger and thumb. Glue the thickest part to the head, securing it in place with the end of a paintbrush. Add a very thin strand of Sugar Dough to the back of the body for the tail.

Black Cat

Using 5g of Black Sugar Dough, make a small cat just as you did for the pigs but, instead of a snout, roll a small ball of pink for the nose. Make the back legs from a small cone shape with a white ball for the foot.

Sheep

1. To complete the sheep you will require 55g of White Sugar Dough and 10g of Black. Take 15g of White for the body and roll into an oval shape. Make a sausage shape with the Black Sugar Dough and cut four legs. Push a piece of raw spaghetti through the centre of each leg and push two into the front of the sheep's body and two into the back.

2. Roll 10g of White Sugar Dough into a cone shape for the head. Push a small piece of dry spaghetti into the body at the front and push the head down over it. Mark the centre of the face with a line and make a smile on either side of this line using tool no. 11.

3. Make the ears from a small amount of White Sugar Dough rolled into two thin cone shapes and line each ear with a little pink. Roll a small ball for the nose and secure in position. Mark the eyes using tool no. 5 or a cocktail stick, and fill with a little ball of Black Sugar Dough.

4. Make the wool by extruding thin strands of White Sugar Dough through the Sugar Dough Press. Cover the body with edible glue and curl the strands as you stick them on. Make three curls to attach to the top of the head. Before securing the sheep to the cake, push a piece of raw spaghetti into the side of the cake and secure the body to it.

Pig

1. Add 5g of Red Sugar Dough to 45g of Flesh Sugar Dough to make the colour required for the pig. Roll 15g into a cone shape for the body and push a piece of raw spaghetti down through the centre, leaving 2cm showing at the top.

2. Roll 5g of Sugar Dough into a cone shape for the back leg, taper it and make it flat at the end, then bend it as shown. Attach to one side of the body. Make the other back leg so that it is folded behind the body. Make the front legs by rolling 10g of Sugar Dough into a sausage shape, make a diagonal cut in the centre then mark the hoof using tool no. 4. Secure to the front of the body with edible glue.

3. For the head, roll 10g into a ball and slip this over the spaghetti at the neck, securing with edible glue. Roll a small ball for the nose, flatten it then stick it to the centre of the face and make two holes for the nostrils. Make a bottom lip by shaping some Sugar Dough into a small banana shape, then glue this under the nose. Mark two small holes for the

eyes and fill with Black Sugar Dough. Roll two small cone shapes for the ears and flatten between your finger and thumb. Attach the thick ends to the head and bend the pointed ends forwards.

4. Using a small blossom cutter, cut out a few flowers from White Sugar

Dough. Fill the centres with a tiny ball of Yellow Sugar Dough and secure these around the pig's neck with edible glue.

Cow

1. To make the cow you will require 15g of pink Sugar Dough (make this by adding 5g of Red Sugar Dough to 10g of White), 50g of White, 5g of Yellow, and 5g of Black Sugar Dough.

2. Roll 15g of White Sugar Dough into a cone shape for the body and push a piece of raw spaghetti down through the centre. Make two back legs by rolling 10g of White Sugar Dough into a sausage shape then make a diagonal cut in the centre and a straight cut at each end. Add four small balls of pink paste, slightly flattened and marked with tool no. 4, for the hoofs. Make two front legs in exactly the same way.

3. Roll a small ball of pink for the udder and add three tiny balls. Secure it to the base of the body using

edible glue. Cut out a few small circles from Black Sugar Dough and glue them to the cow.

4. To make the head, roll 10g of White Sugar Dough into a cone shape. Make a straight cut at the narrowest end. Roll 5g of pink into an oval shape for the nose and glue this to the head then, using the end of a paintbrush, indent two nostrils. Mark the mouth with the edge of a circle cutter. Add two white ears then add two small, cone-shaped horns to the top of the head and a few strands of hair. Fill the eyes with a tiny ball of Black Sugar Dough.

5. For the tail, roll out 5g of White Sugar Dough into a tapered sausage shape, make a tip at the end from Yellow and mark the hair using tool no. 4. Attach the thickest part to the back of the cow and bring the tail forward, in-between the body and the front leg.

Pony

1. To make the pony, you will need 30g of Brown, 10g of Black and 5g of Red Sugar Dough. Make the body and legs from Brown Sugar Dough in the same way as for the cow, omitting the hoofs.

2. Make the head using 10g of Brown Sugar Dough rolled into an oval shape. Push the head over the spaghetti at the neck. Mark two nostrils using the end of a paintbrush and make a smile using the edge of a circle cutter. Roll two small cone shapes for the ears and make a straight cut at the widest part. Glue the ears to either side of the head, using tool no. 1 to push them on. For the eyes, roll two small balls of White Sugar Dough and glue them into position, then add tiny black pupils. Make a bridle from Red Sugar Dough.

3. Make the tail from 5g of Black Sugar Dough, flatten, then mark on the hair using tool, no. 4. Secure to the back of

the pony using edible glue. To make the mane, roll a sausage shape from Black Sugar Dough and mark the hair as before. Glue this to the back of the head and add a small black fringe to the top.

Farmer

1. Roll 30g of Brown Sugar Dough into a cone shape for the body and position on top of the hay cart. Push a piece of raw spaghetti down through the centre and through the hay, leaving 2cm showing at the top. Make a small oval strip and glue it to the front of the body for the trouser flies. Add a small white bib to the top of the body to hide the brown at the neck.

2. Make the legs using 25g of Brown Sugar Dough and shape the knee area.

3. For the boots, darken 20g of Green Sugar Dough with a little Holly/Ivy Paste Food Colour. Roll the Sugar Dough into a sausage shape and cut in half. Bend each piece into an 'L' shape and model the boot, ensuring the rounded end is the toe of the boot. Make two boot soles from 5g of Golden Bear Brown Sugar Dough and attach to the base of the boots with edible glue. Mark the sole and heel with tool no. 4.

4. Mix 10g of White Sugar Dough with a little Blue to make a pale shade, or use a little left over paste from the blue cake covering to make the waistcoat. Roll out and cut a 4cm square for the back. Place onto the back of the body and trim where necessary. Ensure the seams are straight down the side of the body. Roll out the remainder for the front of the waistcoat and roll over it with a textured rolling pin

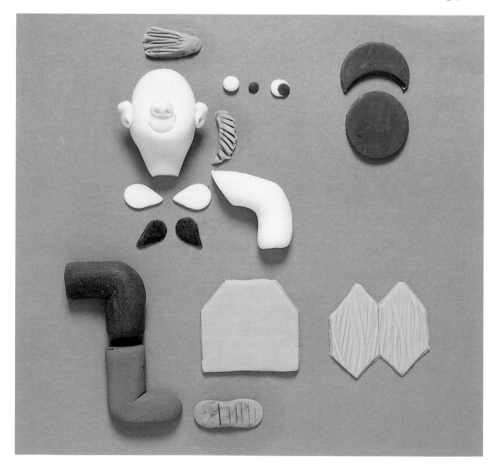

before cutting it out using the template. Stick to the front of the body, joining it neatly at the sides.

5. Roll a ball for the head from 20g of Flesh Sugar Dough then pull out the neck and model the head. For the nose, roll a small cone shape and secure to the centre of the face. Add a big smile using the edge of a circle cutter. Position the eyes and add two small balls of White with a tiny ball of Brown on the top for the pupil. Make some sideburns by rolling a tapered cone shape, flattening it and then marking it with tool no. 4. Place one on each side of the face. Make a quiff by flattening a small cone shape and marking it with the same tool. Stick it to the top of the head and curl it over.

6. Roll a sausage from 15g of White Sugar Dough for the arms, make a diagonal cut in the centre and bend at the elbows. Note that each arm is fitted to the body in a different direction. Secure the arms in position and push a small piece of raw spaghetti into the wrists. You may need to support the right arm with foam until dry. Make the hands from Flesh Sugar Dough and secure to the wrists.

7. Cut out two 2cm circles of Golden Bear Brown Sugar Dough for the cap. Mould one circle for the crown and cut the second circle in half with the cutter for the peak. Stick the two pieces together, allow to dry, and then paint on a check design using Bulrush Liquid Food Colour and a no. 0 paintbrush. Attach the completed cap, using edible glue, to the farmer's right hand.

8. Make two cone shapes from White Sugar Dough for the collar and attach them under the chin. Make two small, red cone shapes for the neckerchief, pinch at the wide end and attach to the collar.

Farmer's Wife

1. Roll 35g of Flesh Sugar Dough into a cone shape. Begin by moulding the narrowest point into a neck and then shape the shoulders and narrow the waist. Pull out the bust with your finger and thumb until you have the required shape.

2. Make the bodice of the dress from 15g of White Sugar Dough. Roll out the paste and cut out a rectangle measuring approximately 10cm x 5cm. Place this on the work surface and position the body over the top. Bring the edges forward, leaving a gap at the bust line and joining neatly at the waist. Make a straight cut at the base of the body and stick to the top of the hay cart.

3. Push a piece of raw spaghetti down through the centre of her torso into the hay cart, leaving 2cm showing at the top to support the head. Push a little piece of spaghetti into the shoulders to support the arms.

4. To make the legs, roll 15g of Flesh Sugar Dough into a sausage and make a diagonal cut in the centre. Shape the legs so that they bend at the knee then make a straight cut just below the knee. Push a piece of raw spaghetti into the end to hold the boot.

5. Make the boots as for the farmer and attach them to the legs. Attach the legs to the side of the body and bend into position. Using a no. 0 paintbrush and some Edelweiss Dust Food Colour mixed with clear alcohol, paint on a few daisies. Add a dot in the centre of each one using Daffodil Dust Food Colour mixed with clear alcohol.

6. For the back of the skirt, roll out 15g of White Sugar Dough and cut out an oval shape measuring approximately 10cm x 3cm. Fold in half loosely along the long edge without creasing it and place the cut edges on the inside, near the back of the body. Place one end in-between the two figures and then bring the other end forward to rest on the side of the hay. This end will be unseen as it will be covered by the front of the skirt.

7. Roll out 25g of White Sugar Dough for the front of the skirt and cut out a rectangle measuring 12cm x 5cm. Gather at the waist and turn under at the hem in soft folds. Glue around the waist and arrange the folds loosely over the legs and to the sides, covering the ends of the back skirt.

8. Divide 20g of White Sugar Dough in half for the sleeves. Roll each piece into a cone shape and mould the top of the sleeve, narrow the arms and bend at the elbow. Apply a little edible glue to the inside of the sleeve and then slip this over the spaghetti at the shoulders. Place one arm behind the farmer's and the other resting on her left leg. Make and position the hands, arranging the fingers on the left hand over the skirt.

9. Make the head from 15g of Flesh Sugar Dough. Roll into a cone and indent the eye area using the side of your little finger. Make a small cone for the nose and glue this into the centre of the face. Make two small nostrils using tool no. 5 or a cocktail stick. Roll two small cone shapes for the ears, place in position and mark a

hole at the base using the end of a paintbrush.

10. Paint on the eyelids and add a wedding band on her finger using a no. 0 paintbrush and some Bulrush Liquid Food Colour mixed with a little Marigold Liquid Food Colour. Shape the bottom lip from Flesh Sugar Dough and stick this to the base of the mouth. Paint on the lips using a no. 0 paintbrush and Poinsettia Liquid Food Colour. Slip the head over the spaghetti at the neck, turning it to face the farmer.

11. Brush the head with edible glue and mix 20g of White Sugar Dough with 5g of Golden Bear Brown Sugar Dough for the hair. Soften it with white vegetable fat so that it will extrude from the sugar shaper easily. Take off a few strands at a time and begin layering the hair from the back of the head to the front.

12. Make a pillbox hat using 10g of White Sugar Dough. Take half the paste, roll it into a ball, flatten it slightly and secure to the top of the head. Roll out the remaining Sugar Dough and cut out two small squares. Fold them in half loosely and attach to each side of the hat using edible glue. Add two small hoop earrings in pink.

13. Dust the cheeks using Cyclamen Dust Food Colour, adding a little Bluebell over the eyelids.

Bouquet

Make a small Mexican hat shape from White Sugar Dough and add a small ball in

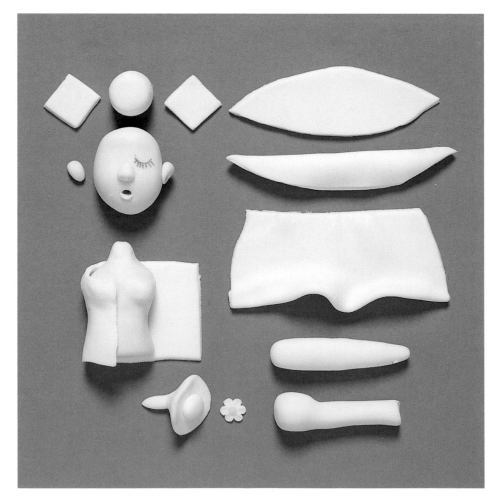

the centre, securing in place with edible glue. Roll out the remaining Sugar Dough, cut out some small blossoms and thin the edges of the petals using the end of a paintbrush. Stick them all around the hat shape and fill each blossom with a dot of Yellow Sugar Dough. Position on the cake and add some ribbon made from Yellow Sugar Dough.

Sheep Dog

1. To make the dog you will need 35g of Black Sugar Dough and 5g of White. Roll 10g of Black Sugar Dough into a cone for the body, then make two smaller cones for the back legs and secure in place. Roll 5g of paste into a sausage for the front legs, make a diagonal cut in the centre and a straight cut at each end. For the back and front paws, roll four balls of White Sugar Dough, attach to the end of each leg and mark the paws using tool no. 4 or the back of a knife.

2. Shape a cone for the head from 6g of Black Sugar Dough and flatten the point. Cut out a leaf shape from White Sugar Dough and glue this onto the centre of the head with the point at the tip of the cone. Smooth the paste over the sides and front of the head. Mark the centre of the face with tool no. 4 and make a small hole for the mouth with the end of a paintbrush.

Mark the fur using tool no. 4 then add a small, black nose.

3. Make the ears by rolling two cone shapes, flatten each one and attach the thickest end to the head, bringing the pointed end forward. Add two small round eyes with pupils.

4. Secure the dog to the cake. Attach a tail to the back of the body and attach the tip of the tail to the hay cart.

Materials

25.5cm (10") round cake

1.5kg (3lb 5oz) white sugarpaste

SK Sugar Dough: 50g (1^3/$_4$oz) Black, 50g (1^3/$_4$oz) Brown, 375g (13^1/$_4$oz) Flesh, 35g (1^1/$_4$oz) Red, 300g (10^1/$_2$oz) White and 30g (1oz) Yellow

SK Paste Food Colour: Teddy Bear Brown

SK Liquid Food Colours: Bulrush, Daffodil and Poinsettia

SK Dust Food Colour: Berberis

SK Designer Dust Colour: Smokey Haze

SK Metallic Lustre Dust: Snowflake

SK Pastel Dust Colour: Baby Blue and Pastel Pink

SK Edible Glue

Raw spaghetti

White vegetable fat

❀

Equipment

33cm (13") round cake drum

Non-stick board and rolling pins: large and small

SK Modelling Tools

SK Spacers and Sizing Cutters

SK Sugar Dough Press

SK Paintbrushes: nos. 00 and 10

Piping bag

Piping nozzle: no. 13

Circle cutters: small (CT)

Templates (see page 104)

Beside the Seaside

As a celebration of summer, I decided to make a cake with a seaside holiday theme. A rather buxom lady, complete with 'Kiss Me Quick' hat, has attracted the attention of a tourist, much to the annoyance of his wife!

Covering the Cake and Board

Colour the white sugarpaste with Teddy Bear Brown Paste Food Colour. Use this paste to cover the board and cake, position the cake in the centre of the board and set aside to dry.

Side Decorations

1. Make three ropes using the leftover sugarpaste from the cake by twisting two long pieces together. Arrange these around the edge of the cake and secure with edible glue.

2. To make the six scalloped, white shells, roll 10g of Sugar Dough for each shell into a cone shape, and then flatten the paste by rolling backwards and forwards with a small rolling pin until you have a fan shape. Using tool no. 4, mark the centre of the shell, and then indent the edges evenly, following the line to the top of the shell. Dust around the edges with Berberis Dust Food Colour.

3. To make the twisted shell, roll 10g of Flesh Sugar Dough into a sausage shape and taper each end. Curl the sausage from one end to the other, making the curls thicker in the centre. Make three and dust with Berberis Dust Food Colour.

Bathing Belle

1. You will require 125g of Flesh Sugar Dough to complete the figure. Begin by dividing 20g of paste in half to make the legs. Roll each piece into a sausage shape and taper slightly at the foot, then roll the knee and ankle area to shape the legs (remember to keep the legs on the chunky side). Shape the foot and mark the toes with tool no. 4. When you have completed each leg, make a diagonal cut on the inside of each leg at the top.

2. Make the body by rolling 30g of Flesh Sugar Dough into a wide cone shape. Roll out some White Sugar Dough and cut out a triangle for the bikini briefs. Glue this into place at the base of the body and then attach the legs, crossing them over at the ankles. Mark a tummy button using tool no. 5.

3. To make the arms, divide 30g of Flesh Sugar Dough in half and roll each piece into a pointed sausage shape. Bend at the elbows and make a diagonal

4. Mix some White and Black Sugar Dough to make approximately 50g of grey paste for the shells. To make the large, grey shell, roll a ball of paste, cup it in the palm of your hand and press the end of a small rolling pin into the centre of the ball to hollow it out. Turn the shape over and pinch it at the edge. Using cutter no. 2 from the spacer and cutter set (3cm), gently mark curved lines from the base to the top. Dust the finished shell with Smokey Haze Designer Dust Colour.

5. To make the small, grey shell, roll a small ball of grey Sugar Dough. Place the ball over the top of tool no. 3 and hollow it out. Pinch the paste on either side to make an oblong shape but keep it open in the centre. Dust the inside and outside with Smokey Haze Designer Dust Colour.

6. Make the starfish by rolling 5g of Flesh Sugar Dough into a ball, then

pinch out five points and roll them to the required length. Prick all over the paste with tool no. 12. Make three.

7. Divide 5g of grey Sugar Dough in half to make two small, cone-shaped shells. Insert the pointed end of tool no. 3 into the thickest end to hollow it out and mark diagonal lines from top to bottom using tool no. 4. Dust on the outside and inside with Smokey Haze Designer Dust Colour. Make six.

8. To make the rounded shells, soften any sugarpaste left over from covering the cake with a little cooled, boiled water. Place a no. 13 piping nozzle into a piping bag, fill with the softened paste and pipe out the shells. Allow to dry.

9. Using a dry no. 10 paintbrush, dust the grey shells with Snowflake Metallic Lustre Dust to give them a silvery finish. Arrange the completed shells in-between the ropes and secure with edible glue.

8. Dust the cheeks with Pastel Pink Dust Colour and brush the eyelids with Baby Blue. Attach the figure to the top of the cake, securing with edible glue.

'Kiss Me Quick' Hat

Roll out 20g of Black Sugar Dough and cut out a 4cm circle for the brim. Roll a ball with the remaining paste and push a 2.5cm circle cutter through the ball to form the crown. Mark the centre with the handle of a paintbrush and glue to the brim. To make the hatband, you can either use a small strip of edible paper with the slogan printed on in edible ink, or cut a strip of Sugar Dough and write on the slogan with a food pen. Dust the hat with Snowflake Metallic Lustre Dust.

Flip Flops

Using three different colours of Sugar Dough, roll an oval shape, flatten between your thumb and finger and glue on top of each other. Make the straps in a 'V' shape and glue in position.

Rocks

To make the rocks you will need 80g of White Sugar Dough and 20g of Black. Use some of each colour to make grey, and then randomly mix the white, black and grey paste together to give a rough stone effect. Make two large rocks for the figures and a smaller one for the seagull.

cut at the shoulder. You do not have to make the fingers as they will be hidden by the head.

4. Divide 5g of Flesh Sugar Dough in half and roll into two balls for the bosom. Push two small pieces of raw spaghetti into the chest area, apply a little glue and secure the bosom in place. Cut out two small triangle shapes for the bikini top and attach in place. Roll a thin lace of White Sugar Dough for the strap and secure this to the bikini top.

5. Roll a ball for the head from 20g of Flesh Sugar Dough. Indent the eye area with your finger. Add an oval ball for the nose and mark the nostrils using tool no. 5. Mark the mouth with a smile using tool no. 11, and then straighten the top lip by inserting tool no. 2. Attach a small banana shape for the bottom lip. Lightly indent the eyelids using tool no. 11. Make two small teardrop shapes for the ears, glue to each side of the head and indent at the

base with a paintbrush. Add two white balls for the earrings. Attach the head to the top of the body, resting on the hands.

6. For the hair, add some Teddy Bear Brown Paste Food Colour to 15g of White Sugar Dough. Soften with a little white vegetable fat and extrude strands of hair through the Sugar Dough Press. Take off a few strands at a time and attach to the head with edible glue. To cover the back of the head, roll a small ball of the same paste, place at the back of the head and mark with tool no. 4.

7. Paint the lips with Poinsettia Liquid Food Colour using a no. 00 paintbrush. Outline the eyelids and paint on the lashes with Bulrush Liquid Food Colour. Paint the earrings, toenails and the stripes on the bikini with Poinsettia Liquid Food Colour.

Husband

1. To make the lower body, roll 20g of Brown Sugar Dough into a ball. Make a straight cut at the top and secure in place on top of the rock.

2. Roll 15g of Brown Sugar Dough into a sausage shape and make a diagonal cut in the centre and a straight cut at each end for the trouser legs. Push a short piece of raw spaghetti into both ends. Make two legs from 15g of Flesh Sugar Dough, bend at the knee and make a straight cut at each end.

3. For the socks, roll 10g of grey Sugar Dough into a sausage shape, turn up at each end for the feet and cut in half. Using tool no. 12, mark the toe of the sock to resemble ribbing. Join the trouser leg, leg and the sock together, and then secure to the body. For the trouser turn-ups, roll a thin sausage shape just long enough to go around the leg. Using a paintbrush, press the handle along the turn-up to mark it.

Brush the back with edible glue and secure around the leg.

4. To make a pair of sandals, roll a small sausage of Brown Sugar Dough to the size of the foot. Flatten the paste between your fingers and glue to the sole of the foot. Add the straps as shown.

5. For the upper body you will need 15g of Flesh Sugar Dough. First, make an oval shape and then pull the neck up at the top and shape the shoulders. Make a straight cut at the bottom. Glue to the lower body on the rock and push a piece of raw spaghetti down through the centre and into the rock, leaving 3cm showing at the top.

6. To make the arms and hands, divide 15g of Flesh Sugar Dough in half. Roll each piece into a sausage shape, shape at the elbow and bend. Flatten the rounded end for the hand and using tool no. 4, mark the thumb and fingers, then roll out slightly to round off the edges. Set aside.

7. Make the vest from 15g of White Sugar Dough. Roll out the paste and cut out two 4.5cm squares for the front and back. Using the template, cut out the neck and armholes. Glue the back and front of the vest to the body, joining at the top of the shoulder and the side seams. Attach the arms and support with foam if necessary.

8. To make the head, roll 15g of Flesh Sugar Dough into a cone shape. Indent the eye area. Roll a small cone for the nose, attach to the face using edible glue, and make the nostrils using tool no. 5. Push the end of a paintbrush into the mouth to make a hole. Add a small banana shape for the lower lip and add a small strip for the upper set of teeth. Make two small, white balls for the eyes and add brown pupils. Paint on the eyebrows using a no. 00 paintbrush and Bulrush Liquid Food Colour. Outline the mouth with diluted Poinsettia Liquid Food Colour. Blush the cheeks with a mixture of Berberis and Pastel Pink Dust Colours. Add a dab to his nose and the top of his ears to make them look sunburnt.

9. Cut out a small square from White Sugar Dough for the handkerchief. Cut each corner and add a tiny ball of paste to resemble a knot and place the handkerchief on top of his head.

10. Make the newspaper from White Sugar Dough rolled out thinly. Carefully fold the paste, apply some edible glue to the palms of the man's hands and place the newspaper over the top, supporting with foam if necessary until dry.

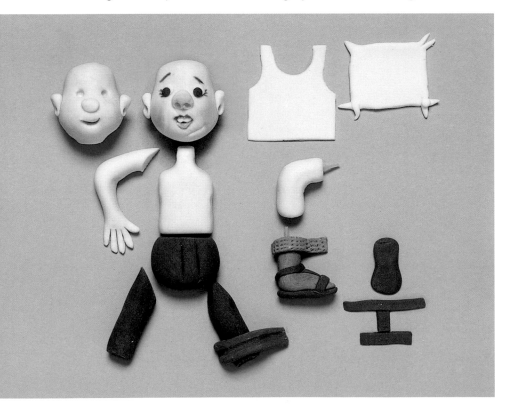

Wife

1. Make the knitting needles by rolling some Red Sugar Dough around two short pieces of raw spaghetti. Add a ball at the end of each needle. Roll out a little Yellow Sugar Dough, cut out a small scarf shape and stitch mark using tool no. 12. Wrap the top around one needle and secure with edible glue.

2. Make the body from 40g of Flesh Sugar Dough as described for the 'bathing belle', but this time pull out the neck in the same way as for the man. Push a piece of raw spaghetti down through the centre, leaving 3cm showing at the top. Make the legs as before from 40g of paste, 15g for the arms and hands and 20g for the head. Assemble in the same order as for the 'bathing belle'.

3. To make the dress, randomly mix together 25g of White Sugar Dough, 15g of Yellow, and 15g of White coloured with a hint of Poinsettia Liquid Food Colour. Using the template as a guide, cut out the front of the dress. Cut out the skirt section of the dress and arrange this into a soft fold, hiding the raw edges. Glue this around the hips, bringing the points forward on each side. These should be hidden by the front of the dress. Secure the front of the dress to the body, adjusting if necessary, and make two straps to cross over at the back.

4. Bend the arms at the elbow and secure to the shoulders. Apply some edible glue to the palms and fingers and wrap them around the knitting needles. To make the ball of wool, roll a small ball of Yellow Sugar Dough and cover it with strands of softened paste extruded through the Sugar Dough Press. Trail a strand of yellow wool from the needles down to the floor.

5. To make the necklace, roll a few small balls of White Sugar Dough and attach each one to the neck with edible glue.

6. Make the head as before from 20g of Flesh Sugar Dough and add the facial features. For the hair, soften 10g of Brown Sugar Dough with white vegetable fat and roll into a ball. Flatten the ball and shape into a cap to fit the head. Attach with edible glue and use tool no. 4 to mark the hair around the head.

7. Make the headband by wrapping a thin strip of the dress colour around the head, making the join at the top. Make two small leaf shapes and a ball for the knot and secure in place. Add a few curls of hair at the front and roll two small, white balls for the earrings.

Beach Bag

1. Roll out 30g of Red Sugar Dough and cut out a 5cm square. Fold and stitch mark the sides. Cut a small rectangle for the pocket, secure to the front of the bag and stitch mark on three sides. Make a small, white rope for the handles.

2. Make a small towel from White Sugar Dough, cut a fringe at one end and roll up. Make a small bottle from a tiny piece of any colour and put the bottle and towel into the bag.

Seagull

Roll 20g of White Sugar Dough into a cone shape for the body. Pull out the neck and shape the head and beak. To make the wings, divide 10g of paste in half, roll each piece into a cone shape and flatten the curved edge. Mark the feathers using tool no. 4. Paint the beak with Daffodil Liquid Food Colour and dust the wings with Smokey Haze Designer Dust. Attach the bird to the rock and add the claws to finish.

Materials

12.5cm and 15cm (5" and 6") round
cakes

800g (1lb 12oz) white sugarpaste

SK Sugar Dough: 30g (1oz) Brown, 350g
(12oz) Golden Bear Brown and 350g
(12oz) White

SK Paste Food Colour: Berberis

SK Dust Food Colour: Poinsettia

SK Edible Glue

❀

Equipment

20.5cm (8") round cake drum

Non-stick board and rolling pin

SK Modelling Tools

SK Spacers and Sizing Cutters

SK Paintbrush: no. 2

Circle cutters: small (CT)

Leaf cutters (optional) (PME)

Square cutters: small (CT)

Sugar shaper with trefoil disc

Ribbed rolling pin (PME)

Textured rolling pin

Cocktail stick

Cake dowels

Templates (see page 105)

She Caught Her Man

You have héard of the gingerbread man who boasted he ran so fast that no one could catch him, well obviously this one didn't run fast enough and so he has ended up at the alter! This informal design is perfect for the couple who are searching for an unconventional wedding cake.

Covering the Cakes and Board

1. Colour 800g of sugarpaste with Berberis Paste Food Colour. Cover both cakes and set aside to dry.

2. Use the Berberis coloured sugarpaste to cover the board. Decorate the board edges using a textured rolling pin. Secure the larger cake to the centre of the board and set the smaller cake aside. Dowel the larger cake if necessary (see page 9). Keep the leftover pieces of coloured paste for later use.

Gingerbread People

1. Roll out 125g of Golden Bear Brown Sugar Dough between the spacers with the grooves facing upwards, ensuring you have an even finish. Cut out seven gingerbread figures, one at a time, using the template. Smooth out any rough edges by dipping your finger into a little cooled, boiled water and running it along the areas that need smoothing.

Dressing the Gingerbread People

The easiest way to do this is to cut out a square of Sugar Dough, lay this on top of the figure and mark the size and shape you require then remove the piece and trim it neatly to fit. The figures are described going around the cake in an anti-clockwise direction, beginning with the gingerbread man at the front of the cake.

Figure A

1. Cut out a rectangle of White Sugar Dough for the shirt front measuring approximately 3cm x 2cm and taper this by narrowing the sides. Mark the stitching down the centre and down either side using tool no. 12 then use edible glue to stick it to the front of the body.

2. Roll out a small piece of Brown Sugar Dough and cut out the lapels using a leaf cutter (or using the template). Cut the leaf in half lengthways and glue a lapel on either side of the shirt

2. Use tool no. 4 to mark a smile on the faces and make two small holes for the eyes using tool no. 5. Fill the eyes with tiny balls of Brown Sugar Dough and brush the cheeks with Poinsettia Dust Food Colour. Set aside to dry.

3. Mark out seven points around the side of the larger cake where the gingerbread people will be attached when completed (see page 9).

Rolling Pin and Wooden Spoon

1. Roll 10g of Golden Bear Brown Sugar Dough into a ball and then into a sausage shape. Use tool no. 5 to mark a line around either end of the rolling pin.

2. Roll 5g of Golden Bear Brown Sugar Dough into a sausage shape. Press your finger into one end to form the spoon shape and make a line around the top using tool no. 4. Press a small hole into the top of the handle using a cocktail stick.

3. Decorate the spoon and rolling pin with thin strips of White Sugar Dough for ribbons and bows. To make a horseshoe, cut out a 2cm circle and then cut out the middle with a smaller circle cutter. Attach the horseshoe to the rolling pin on the end of a thin strip of White Sugar Dough.

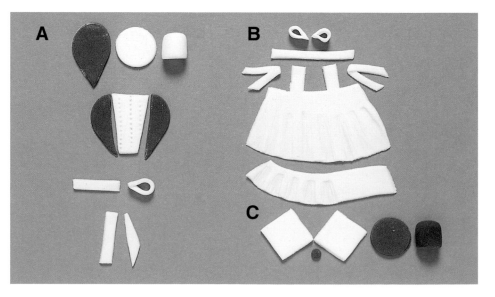

front. Add three small, white buttons down the front.

3. For the hat, roll out some White Sugar Dough and cut out a 2cm circle. For the top, roll a small ball, flatten it with your fingers then attach it to the brim with edible glue. Roll out a small piece of the Berberis coloured sugarpaste for the hatband and wrap it around the hat to cover the join. Secure the completed hat to the head. Make a small bow with tails from White Sugar Dough and attach this to the top of the shirt. Stick the completed figure to the side of the cake.

Figure B

1. Roll out a strip of White Sugar Dough for the petticoat measuring 8cm x 1.5cm. Frill the lower edge with a cocktail stick. Place this over the figure and trim off any excess length then attach to the body with edible glue.

2. Cut out a 5cm x 7cm rectangle from White Sugar Dough for the dress. Take out a small square for the neckline at the top and cut off the corners on either side. Using a cocktail stick, frill the skirt and taper the sides then trim the length if required and attach to the body.

3. Cut two short narrow strips of White Sugar Dough and fold over for the ties on the shoulders. Make a headband using another strip and add a small bow to the band then use edible glue to attach it across the head.

Figure C

1. Roll out and cut two squares, measuring about 2cm, to make a waistcoat. Cut off one corner from each square

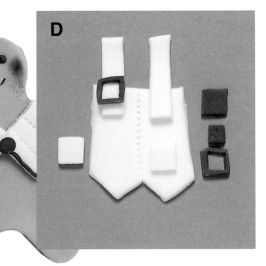

and attach these to the body on the diagonal, crossing them over at the front. Mark the stitching diagonally across the squares and add a small Brown Sugar Dough ball for the button. Roll a very thin shoelace of Brown Sugar Dough to edge the waistcoat.

2. Make the hat in Brown Sugar Dough in the same way as for figure A.

Figure D

1. Make the white dungarees by cutting out a 4cm square from White Sugar Dough. Mark the stitches down the centre and then cut two 'V' shapes in the lower edge.

2. Cut along the sides at an angle then cut out two small square pockets and attach these to the front, marking stitch mark on three sides. Adjust the length at the top edge if necessary and then fix the dungarees into position.

3. Add two narrow shoulder straps. Make two brown buckles from two 1cm squares of Brown Sugar Dough, remove the middle with a smaller square cutter and add a small strip down the centre.

Figure E

1. To make the bodice, cut out a 2cm x 3cm rectangle from White Sugar Dough and cut the neckline using a small

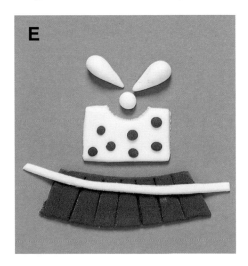

circle cutter. Attach to the top of the figure and add a few Brown Sugar Dough dots for decoration.

2. Roll out a strip of Brown Sugar Dough for the skirt measuring 6cm x 2cm. Mark the pleats by pressing tool no. 4 into the Sugar Dough. Attach to the body, adding a thin strip of White for the belt.

3. Make a bow for the hair by rolling two small cone shapes of White Sugar Dough. Stick these to the head and add a small ball in the centre.

Figure F

1. To make the t-shirt, cut out an oblong shape measuring approximately 4cm x 2.5cm then create the neckline using a small circle cutter. Cut off the lower corners and secure to the body with edible glue. Add two small Brown Sugar Dough balls for the buttons on the shoulders.

2. Cut out a rectangle from Brown Sugar Dough, measuring 4cm x 3cm for the trousers. Mark the centre with stitch marks and cut a 'V' shape from the lower edge. Make a diagonal cut on each side and add stitch marks to the lower edge. Attach them to the body with edible glue.

3. Make the hat using Brown Sugar Dough as before.

Figure G

1. To make the skirt for the white dress, roll out a strip measuring 11cm x 4cm. Gather the piece at the top to fit the width of the body and secure it in place with edible glue. Make the frill at the top from a piece measuring 11cm x 1.5cm. Frill once again and flatten the top edge to reduce the bulk. Attach over the top of the skirt.

2. Cut out the hat with a 3cm circle cutter then apply some edible glue

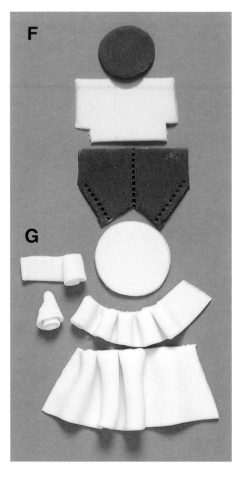

and arrange it from the back of the head to the brim at the front. Trim with a small rose made by rolling up a narrow strip of Sugar Dough. Open out at the top edge and squeeze at the base. Secure to the hat with a little edible glue.

White Picket Fence

1. Roll out 250g of White Sugar Dough between the spacers and run the ribbed rolling pin over the top to make the lines on the fencing. Cut out four strips measuring 25cm x 1cm and then fix two of these horizontally around the side of the smaller cake, joining them neatly at each side. Secure the other two strips 1.5cm above the first set. Cut out more strips for the fence posts, this time measuring 7cm x

1cm. Make a point at the top of each post and stick them evenly around the cake.

2. To make the draped decoration at the top of the fence you will need to fill a sugar shaper with White Sugar Dough softened with white vegetable fat. Insert the trefoil disc then extrude a long piece and arrange it in drapes around the top of the fence. Make small bow shapes and secure them to the fence posts with edible glue. Set the top tier aside until dry and then secure it to the bottom tier.

Groom

1. Using the template, cut out a large gingerbread figure as before then mark the eyes and smile.

2. Turn the groom over and dress him from the back. Cut out the tailcoat using the template and adjust accordingly to fit the figure. The bottom of the tails should be longer than the body so that they rest on the cake surface where he is standing; this will help to hold him in place.

3. Turn the figure over to dress the front. Cut out a rectangle measuring 3cm x 4cm for the waistcoat and mark the

3. Make the sleeves by cutting out two 2.5cm circles, frill all around the edges with a cocktail stick and then fold each one in half. Attach one to each shoulder then make two ties to hang down the back of the dress.

4. To make the hat, frill a 2.5cm circle and a 1.5cm circle. Place the small circle on top of the larger one and secure to the head with edible glue.

Finishing Touches

Carefully place the top tier in place, ensuring you do not damage the fence or the gingerbread people. Secure the rolling pin and the spoon to the top of the cake with edible glue.

stitching down the centre using tool no. 12. Cut out an inverted 'V' shape at the base of the stitch marks. Roll out some White Sugar Dough and, using a leaf cutter or the template as a guide, make the lapels in the same way as before. Use edible glue to secure them to the edge of the shirt.

4. Make a small collar from a strip of White Sugar Dough measuring 2.5cm x 1cm. Make a diagonal cut at each end and a small cut in the centre. Stick to the top of the waistcoat and turn the ends over. Add two small tails for his tie and three buttons.

5. Stand the groom upright and position him on top of the cake so that he will be looking towards his bride, ensuring that you leave enough room for her stand beside him. He may need to be supported with foam until dry.

6. Make a small top hat from White Sugar Dough with a Berberis coloured hatband. Secure the hat in place using edible glue.

Bride

1. Cut out the bride using the large template, as for the groom. Roll out some White Sugar Dough and cut out a rectangle measuring 6cm x 5cm then cut out the dress shape using the template. Frill the edges of the sleeves using a cocktail stick then attach the dress to the body and secure the figure to the top of the cake with edible glue. Leave to dry before dressing the back.

2. For the back of the dress, cut out a 6cm circle and make a straight cut at the top. Gather this edge to fit the width of the body and secure with edible glue. Add a thin, white strip for the waistband then make a frill from a strip of White Sugar Dough measuring 12cm x 1.5cm. Secure the frill around the edge of the skirt with edible glue; this will help to support the figure.

At the Barre

Ballerinas often grace celebration cakes as they are so popular with little girls. This cake could be made to celebrate a birthday or dancing exam success, or to wish a young dancer good luck before a performance.

Materials

15cm (6") hexagonal cake

1.1kg (2lb 7oz) white sugarpaste

SK Sugar Dough: 270g (9^1/$_2$oz) Black, 140g (5oz) Brown, 270g (9^1/$_2$oz) Flesh, 30g (1oz) Golden Bear Brown, 200g (7oz) White

SK Paste Food Colours: Berberis, Bluebell, Chestnut, Sunflower and Teddy Bear Brown

SK Pastel Dust Colours: Baby Blue and Pastel Pink

SK Magic Sparkle Dust

SK Liquid Food Colours: Bulrush, Daffodil and Fuchsia

SK Edible Glitter Flakes: Silver

SK Edible Glue

SK Gildesol

Raw spaghetti

White vegetable fat

Equipment

30.5cm (12") hexagonal cake drum

Non-stick board and rolling pin

SK Modelling Tools

SK Spacers and Sizing Cutters

SK Sugar Dough Press

SK Paintbrushes: nos. 0 and 10

Carnation cutter 4cm (1^1/$_2$") (available from SK)

Circle cutters: small (CT)

Lacy heart cutter set: LH3 (OP)

Scriber or cocktail stick

Template (see page 105)

Covering the Cake and Board

1. Colour 500g of sugarpaste with a hint of Berberis Paste Food Colour to make a pale shade. Cover the cake and secure it centrally on the board.

2. Colour 500g of sugarpaste with Teddy Bear Brown Paste Food Colour. Roll out and cut a strip measuring 20.5cm x 7.5cm and place it along the edge of the board. Cut a second strip and place it along the next edge with the paste overlapping at the corner. Using a sharp knife, cut diagonally through both layers from the corner of the board to the cake. Remove the piece underneath to leave a mitred join. Continue around the board until you have all the sections covered.

Star

Roll out 100g of white sugarpaste and, using the template as a guide, cut out the star and soften the edges before securing to the top of the cake with edible glue. Apply a thin coat of Gildesol to the surface of the star with a soft brush and then dust with Silver Edible Glitter Flakes.

The Barre

Add a little Chestnut Paste Food Colour to 30g of Golden Bear Brown Sugar Dough. Do not blend the colour in completely: this will achieve wood grain effect. Roll the paste into a sausage and cut into six lengths, each measuring 7cm. Glue these to each side of the cake, supporting with foam until dry.

Prima Ballerina

1. Colour 50g of White Sugar Dough with Bluebell Paste Food Colour. Roll 15g of this paste into a cone shape for the body and then cut off the top third at the narrow end. Position the lower body in the centre of the star on top of the cake and secure with edible glue.

2. To make the upper body, roll 5g of Flesh Sugar Dough into a small cone shape. Pinch and smooth the pointed end at the top to create the neck and model the shoulders. Secure the shoulders to the lower body using edible glue and push a piece of raw spaghetti down into the neck and body, leaving 3cm showing at the top.

3. Roll 25g of White Sugar Dough into a sausage shape for the legs and divide equally. Shape the rounded ends into the ballet shoes. Narrow the paste at the ankle and knee to shape the legs and then attach the legs into position with edible glue. Bend the legs at the knees and cross the right leg over the left. Paint on the shoes using Baby Blue Pastel Dust Colour mixed with clear alcohol. Alternatively, you may prefer to paint on the shoes before you secure the legs to the body.

4. For the skirt, roll out the remaining blue paste to a thickness of 2mm and cut out three layers for the skirt using the carnation cutter. Lightly roll over each layer to make the shape slightly larger, and then using a cocktail stick or tool no. 5, thin the edges to make a pretty frill. Cut out the centre of each using a small circle cutter and slip the skirts over the body. Support each layer with thick pieces of foam to lift the paste.

5. To make the decoration for the front of the bodice, roll out a little White Sugar Dough and cut out the lace shape. Lift out the design and, using one section only, carefully remove the centres using a scriber or cocktail stick. Apply the design to the front of the bodice with edible glue.

6. Make the arms from Flesh Sugar Dough, narrow the paste at the wrist and elbow and flatten the hand slightly. Cut the thumb and fingers and round off the edges. Attach to the shoulders using edible glue and bring the arms forward to rest on the left leg, placing one on top of the other. Add small, white straps to cover the join at the shoulder.

7. Roll 10g of Flesh Sugar Dough into a cone shape for the head and indent the eye area. Roll a tiny oval shape for the nose and secure in the centre of the face with edible glue. Using tool no. 1, lightly mark a smile and two eyelids. Mix a little Daffodil Liquid Food Colour with Bulrush and add the eyebrows and eyelashes using a no. 0 paintbrush. Paint on the mouth using Fuchsia Liquid Food Colour. Finally, add two small teardrop shapes for the ears and attach to the side of the head using edible glue. Indent the ears with the end of a paintbrush. Apply a little glue to the neck area and slip the head over the top.

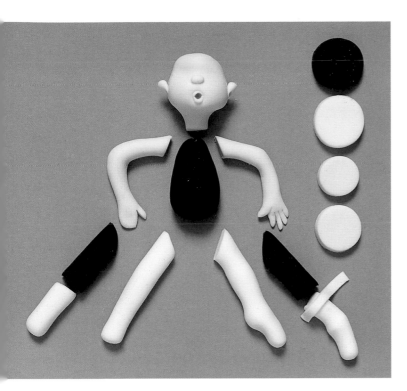

8. Brush the head with edible glue. Colour 25g of White Sugar Dough with Sunflower Paste Food Colour and soften with a little white vegetable fat. Fill the cup of the Sugar Dough Press and extrude the hair. Take of a few strands at a time and begin to layer the hair. To make the topknot, take three or four longer strands and twist them round into a bun, then secure to the head with glue.

9. Using a soft, dry brush, dust the cheeks with Pastel Pink Dust Food Colour and the eyelids with a mixture of Baby Blue Pastel Dust Food Colour and Magic Sparkle Dust.

10. Using a soft, dry brush, apply some Gildesol around the edges of the tutu and ballet shoes and dust with Magic Sparkle Dust.

Ballet Students

1. Use the Spacers and Sizing Cutters set to proportion the ballerinas. Following the step photograph as a guide,

make the body from Black Sugar Dough using cutter no. 3, the head and neck from Flesh or Brown Sugar Dough using cutter no. 3, the arms from the same colour as the head using cutter no. 2 and the legs from either White Sugar Dough or Black Sugar Dough with White legwarmers from cutter no. 3. Assemble the parts using edible glue and arrange the figures in different positions.

2. Create different facial expressions for each figure (see pages 14 to 15) and various hairstyles using different shades of Sugar Dough extruded through the Sugar Dough Press. Paint on the ballet shoes and any extra detail and allow to dry before securing the figures to the board.

Materials

20.5cm (8") square cake

1.4kg (3lb 1oz) white sugarpaste

SK Sugar Dough: 35g (1¼oz) Black, 10g (⅓oz) Brown, 35g (1¼oz) Flesh, 85g (3oz) Golden Bear Brown, 15g (½oz) Green, 20g (¾oz) Orange, 40g (1½oz) Red, 480g (1lb 1oz) White and 15g (½oz) Yellow

SK Paste Food Colours: Bluebell and Thrift

SK Dust Food Colour: Thrift

SK Metallic Lustre Dust: Silver

SK Pastel Dust Colour: Baby Blue

SK Liquid Food Colours: Blackberry, Bluebell, Bulrush, Daffodil and Poinsettia

220g (7¾oz) SK Instant Mix Pastillage

SK Edible Glue

SK Confectioners' Glaze

Raw spaghetti

White vegetable fat

Clear alcohol

❁

Equipment

25.5cm (10") square cake drum

20.5cm (8") round cake dummy

Non-stick board and rolling pin

SK Modelling Tools

SK Spacers and Sizing Cutters

SK Sugar Dough Press

SK Paintbrushes: nos. 00 and 0

Circle cutters: small (CT)

Sandpaper (new)

Floppy mat (SC)

Templates (see page 104)

Kitchen Capers

This cake is a tribute to the television chefs who entertain us with their recipes, but you can, of course, make it for a food lover in your own family.

Covering the Cake and Board

Roll out 600g of white sugarpaste and cover the board. Colour the remaining sugarpaste with Bluebell Paste Food Colour and cover the cake. Place the cake centrally on the board.

Tumbling Chefs

1. To make the 12 small chefs, roll out 60g of White Sugar Dough into a strip. Cut the strip neatly to measure 21cm x 2.5cm. Cut out 12 triangles for the bodies and place under a floppy mat to keep moist.

2. For the arms, roll out 60g of White Sugar Dough and cut a strip measuring 16cm x 2cm. Cut out 24 slices for the arms and place under a mat. Repeat the same procedure for the legs, making them slightly wider than the arms.

3. Roll out 25g of Flesh Sugar Dough and cut out 12 x 2cm circles for the head, then place under the floppy mat.

4. To make the shoes, roll out 25g of White Sugar Dough and cut out 12 x 2cm circles. Cut each circle in half to make two shoes and place under the mat until required.

5. To make sure that all the chefs are the same size, mark out a rectangle measuring 7cm x 8cm on a silver cake board and construct each chef within the rectangle. First, place the triangle into the middle of the square. Take two legs, make a diagonal cut at the top of each and glue them to the edge of the body. Add two semi-circles for shoes. Make a diagonal cut on the arms and secure to the body.

6. Secure the head to the top of the body. Using tool no. 5, mark two holes for the eyes, and mark a smile using tool no. 11. Do not add a nose. Fill the eyes with tiny balls of Black Sugar Dough, then make the moustache and secure the pieces into place with edible glue.

7. For the hats, roll out 25g of White Sugar Dough and cut out 12 x 2cm circles. Make a straight cut at the edge and secure to the head. Add a thin strip for the hatband.

8. Cut out two red leaf shapes for the neckerchief and secure into place, then add a small ball for the knot. Using tool no. 5, mark some buttons off-centre down the front of the jacket.

9. Paint the trousers using a no. 0 paintbrush and either Blackberry, Bluebell or Poinsettia Liquid Food Colour. Allow to dry before attaching the chefs to the cake. For each side, place the first chef in the centre and one on either side. Finally, add the hands and secure in place with edible glue.

Counter

1. Mix up 220g of pastillage following the directions on the packet. Roll out 75g and cut out a curved piece for the top of the counter, using the template as a guide. Roll out a further 75g of pastillage and cut out two side pieces measuring 6.5cm x 4cm. Place all three pieces on a

flat, non-stick surface. Cut out a rectangle for the front of the counter to measure 7cm x 16cm. Stand a 20.5cm round cake dummy on its side, and place this piece over it to dry. Leave all the pieces for 12 hours before turning them over to dry the other side. After 12 hours, stand the front of the counter upright and allow to dry for a further 12 hours.

Once all the pieces are dry, mix a strong

2. glue consisting of clear alcohol and pastillage powder to a cream consistency. Smooth any rough edges from the pastillage pieces with fine sandpaper, apply the strong glue to the edges and assemble the counter upside down. Leave in this position until the glue is dry before turning it upright. Paint the counter inside and out with a mixture of Bulrush and Daffodil Liquid Food Colours and set aside to dry. Paint the top of the counter with Baby Blue Pastel Dust Colour mixed with a little clear alcohol.

3. Make a hanging rail at both sides and along the front of the counter from Golden Bear Brown Sugar Dough. Use tool no. 3 to mark the position of the hanging hooks.

4. To make the three tea towels, roll out 25g of White Sugar Dough and cut out three 5cm squares. Paint a check design on two and fringe the other. Fold them into a natural hanging position. Where you have marked the rail, add a

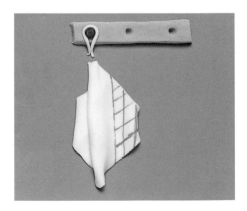

small ball of Brown Sugar Dough and add a white hanging loop over the top. Glue the tea towel directly underneath the brown ball, covering the ends of the hanging loop.

Utensils

1. Make the wooden spoon and rolling pin from Golden Bear Brown Sugar Dough. Hang these on the right of the chef with one tea towel.

2. Model the oven glove from Orange Sugar Dough and add two rows of stitch marks using tool no. 12. Hang this beside two tea towels on the left of the chef.

3. For the spatula, roll a small sausage shape of grey Sugar Dough, flatten the lower half and round off the top for the handle and shape by it rolling in-between your fingers. Using the end of a paintbrush, make a hole in the top of the handle. Dust with Silver Metallic Lustre Dust and then glue it to the hanging rail at the front of the counter. Place a brown ball inside the hole at the top and secure with edible glue.

4. Model the fish slice from grey Sugar Dough and mark holes using tool no. 5. Make a hole in the top as before and hang at the opposite end of the rail.

5. To make the saucepan, you will require 20g of grey Sugar Dough. Roll out the paste to a thickness of 5mm and cut out a 2.5cm circle for the base. Cut a strip measuring 9cm x 2cm and glue this around the circle, make a neat join and secure with edible glue. Roll out the handle into a sausage shape and flatten the end, then glue this over the seam on the side of the saucepan. Support the handle with foam until dry, and then dust with Silver Metallic Lustre Dust. Apply some glue to the rim of the pan and the handle, and then place it over the hanging rail, pressing it to the front of the counter. Add the brown ball into the hole in the handle.

6. Make the frying pan in exactly the same way, but reduce the width of the strip for the sides. Secure in place.

7. Roll out 10g of Golden Bear Brown Sugar Dough and cut out a

rectangle for the chopping board measuring 4cm x 3cm. Glue this to the top of the counter.

8. To make the colander, cut out a 3cm circle from White Sugar Dough and prick it with tool no. 5. Roll a small ball of White Sugar Dough and place this underneath to raise the centre. Glue a small strip and glue around the top and add two small handles. Apply edible glue around the edges and secure to the counter.

9. Make the chef's knife from grey Sugar Dough and then set aside to dry.

10. Roll a sausage of Yellow Sugar Dough for the oil bottle and narrow the top half. Mark the cork with tool no. 4 and add a small white label.

11. Make the pestle and mortar from 10g of White Sugar Dough. Roll 8g of paste into a ball and hollow it out using tool no. 3. Shape the base using your fingers. Make a small cone shape, mark the top and glue this inside the bowl.

12. To make a terracotta bowl for the vegetables, roll 20g of Golden Bear Brown Sugar Dough into a ball, hollow out the centre with the end of a small rolling pin, open the rim and then narrow and shape the bottom. Set aside to dry.

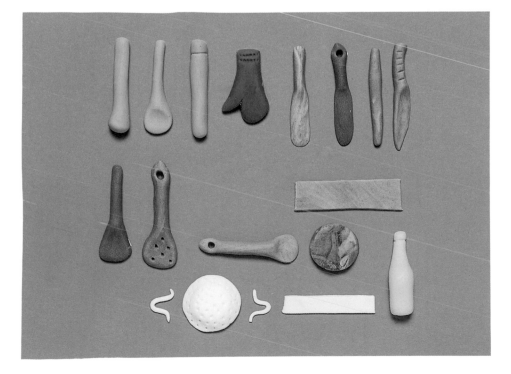

Vegetables

1. **Carrots:** divide 10g of Orange Sugar Dough into four equal pieces and mould into tapered cone shapes. Indent the top with tool no. 3 and add a small green stalk. Mark the carrot with tool no. 4. Glue one carrot to the chopping board and chop off three sections from the bottom.

2. **Mushrooms:** divide 5g of White Sugar Dough into three equal pieces. Roll each piece into a ball for the mushroom heads and flatten with your finger. Roll a small ball of Brown Sugar Dough for the underside and mark with a knife, secure to the head with edible glue and then add the stalk.

3. **Turnip:** roll 5g of White Sugar Dough into a ball, pull out a point at the base, indent the other end using tool no. 3 and mark the skin with horizontal lines. Insert a small stalk and dust with Thrift Dust Food Colour.

4. **Garlic:** roll 5g of White Sugar Dough into a ball, pull out to a point at the base and indent the other end using tool no. 3. Mark in sections with tool no. 4 and dust with Thrift Dust Food Colour.

5. **Tomatoes:** roll two balls of Red Sugar Dough and indent the top of each using tool no. 3. Add a stalk made from Green Sugar Dough.

6. **Peas in the pod:** make two banana shapes from 5g of Green Sugar Dough and flatten with your fingers. Roll some peas and glue on top of one pod. Place the other pod on the top, allowing the peas to show.

7. **Aubergines:** colour 15g of White Sugar Dough with Thrift Paste Food Colour. Divide in half and roll two soft cone shapes. Indent each end with tool no. 8. Make three small leaves and a stalk from Green Sugar Dough and insert the stalk at the top with the leaves.

8. **Yellow peppers:** make two of these from Yellow Sugar Dough in the same way as for the carrot, but taper the ends to a finer point.

9. **Lemons:** roll two balls of Yellow Sugar Dough and pull the ends out slightly. Prick all over with a cocktail stick.

10. **Corn:** add 2g of Yellow Sugar Dough to 5g of White and mix together to make a pale yellow. Make a tapered cone shape and roll small balls in lines from the top to bottom until it is covered. Make the leaves by adding a little Green Sugar Dough to the corn colour you have been using to make a light green. Roll a thin, tapered leaf shape, flatten lightly with a rolling pin and mark with tool no. 4. Make one large leaf and add three smaller ones.

11. **Artichoke:** add a little Thrift Paste Food Colour to 5g of Green Sugar Dough. Make a small cone shape for the base, apply some glue to the surface and begin at the top by layering small leaf shapes in an alternate pattern until the cone is covered.

12. Once everything is complete, arrange the vegetables on the top of the counter and secure in position.

Chef

1. Divide 10g of Black Sugar Dough in half and roll two ovals for the shoes. Make the soles from Golden Bear Brown Sugar Dough and secure to the shoes.

2. To make the legs, roll 40g of White Sugar Dough into a sausage shape, make a diagonal cut in the centre and trim each leg to measure 5cm long. Apply some edible glue to the top of the shoes and push a piece of raw spaghetti down through each leg and into the top of the shoe, leaving 3cm showing at the top of the legs.

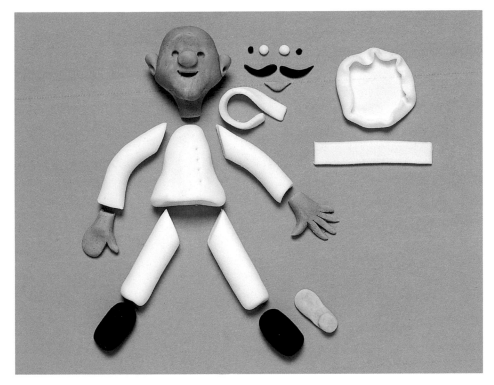

3. Paint the trousers in a check design using a no. 00 paintbrush and some Blackberry Liquid Food Colour. Allow to dry.

4. Make the top of the chef by rolling 25g of White Sugar Dough into a cone shape. Hollow out a little at the base and apply some glue inside. Slip the body over the spaghetti at the top of the legs. Push another piece of raw spaghetti down through the body, leaving 3cm showing at the neck.

5. Add 5g of Brown Sugar Dough to 20g of Teddy Bear Brown to make the flesh colour. Roll 20g of this paste into a ball for the head. Pull out the neck and then indent the eye area with the side of your finger. Add a small cone shape for the nose and mark the nostrils. Using tool no. 11, mark a smile and then straighten out the top lip by inserting the small end of tool no. 10. Add a small, white banana shape for the teeth and mark and a small, flesh-coloured banana shape for the bottom lip. Add the eyes, eyebrows and ears. Finally, add two small, curved cone shapes

made from Black Sugar Dough for the moustache and secure under the nose using edible glue. Allow to dry.

6. Apply some edible glue around the neck area and slip the head over the raw spaghetti. Cut a small strip of white for the collar and attach in place. Add some buttons down the front of the jacket.

7. To make the chef's hat, roll out 20g of White Sugar Dough. Cut out a 4cm circle and turn the edges inwards. Roll out a strip for the hatband, glue this in a circle on top of the head and place the hat on the top.

8. Soften 10g of Black Sugar Dough with white vegetable fat and fill the cup of a Sugar Dough Press. Extrude very short strands of hair, chop them off and then arrange them around the back of the head and over the ears.

9. Apply some edible glue to the soles of the chef's shoes and stand the chef in the desired position behind the counter before you attach the arms.

10. For his arms, roll 25g of White Sugar Dough into a sausage shape, make a diagonal cut in the centre and a straight cut at each end. Bend each arm at the elbow and attach to the shoulders. They should reach the counter top.

11. Make the hands from the flesh-coloured paste, slip a short piece of raw spaghetti into the wrists and glue the fingers of the right hand around the chef's knife. Attach the hands to the sleeve securely. The knife should be near the chopped carrot on the board.

Finishing Touches

Make the vegetables shine by giving them a coat of confectioners' glaze, leave the first coat to dry and then apply a second.

Materials

20.5cm (8") round cake

1kg (2lb 3oz) white sugarpaste

SK Sugar Dough: 10g ($^1/_3$oz) Blue, 1kg (2lb 3oz) Golden Bear Brown, 10g ($^1/_3$oz) Red, 400g (14oz) White

SK Dust Food Colours: Bluebell, Daffodil, Edelweiss, Leaf Green, Nasturtium and Rose

SK Paste Food Colours: Bulrush and Marigold

SK Liquid Food Colours: Bluebell, Bulrush, Mint and Poinsettia

SK Magic Sparkle Dust

100g (3$^1/_2$oz) SK Instant Mix Pastillage

SK Edible Glue

SK Gildesol

Raw spaghetti

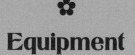

Equipment

30.5cm (12") round cake drum

Non-stick board and rolling pin

SK Modelling Tools

SK Spacers and Sizing Cutters

SK Paintbrush: no. 0

Circle cutters: small (CT)

Cocktail sticks

Templates (see page 105)

Just Bears

Every child loves their teddy bear and they are so easy to make in sugar. To personalise this cake you could make the letters to spell the birthday boy or girl's name.

Covering the Cake and Board

Roll out 650g of white sugarpaste to cover the cake. Roll out the remaining white sugarpaste to cover the board. Attach the cake to the board and set aside to dry.

Making the Letters

1. Roll out 180g of White Sugar Dough between two spacers. Cut out the five letters using the templates. Mix a small amount of Edelweiss Dust Food Colour with Bluebell, Nasturtium, Daffodil, Rose and Leaf Green Dust Food Colours to create a paler shade of each colour, then dust these colours over the letters.

> **TIP** To seal the dust onto the letters, pass them quickly and carefully over a steaming kettle after they have been dusted. This will prevent the dust from marking your fingers and the white sugarpaste on the cake. Take extra care to ensure you do not scald your hands.

2. Set the letters aside to firm slightly, and then fix them to the side of the cake with edible glue. Position the letter 'A' at the front of the cake in the centre then stick the other letters in position.

3. You will need 75g of Golden Bear Brown Sugar Dough for the teddy bears on the letters. Model five heads and add the some Golden Bear Brown Sugar Dough mixed with White Sugar Dough for the cheeks. Shape the paws and roll a small oval shape of White Sugar Dough to stick on their back paws for the pads. Paint a pattern on the pads with a no. 0 paintbrush and various different Liquid Food Colours. Allow to dry.

4. Secure all the parts to the letters using edible glue. Fill in the eyes and noses with tiny balls of Golden Bear Brown Sugar Dough mixed with Bulrush Paste Food Colour.

Table

1. Roll out 100g of pastillage using the spacers with the grooves facing upwards. Cut out a 5cm circle and leave this to dry on a non-stick surface. Roll the remainder of the pastillage into a sausage shape for the pedestal: it needs to be approximately 2cm in diameter and 5cm long. Make a straight cut at each end and push a piece of raw spaghetti

down through the centre, leaving one end protruding. Leave this to dry in an upright position. After a few hours, turn the circle over to dry the other side.

2. Once the two pieces are dry, place the circle onto the work surface and stick the pedestal in the centre, pushing the spaghetti through the centre of the circle and leaving a little showing to push the cake onto later. Stick the table onto the cake top with edible glue.

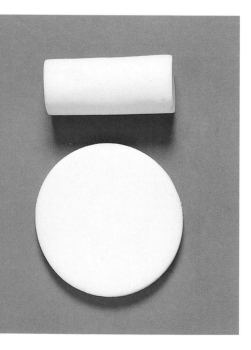

3. Roll out 75g of White Sugar Dough and cut out an 18cm circle for the tablecloth. Frill the edge with a cocktail stick and then dust the frills with Rose Dust Food Colour. Apply some edible glue to the top of the table and lay the Sugar Dough tablecloth over it, arranging the folds down the sides.

Birthday Cake

1. Mix 15g of White Sugar Dough with 5g of Blue Sugar Dough to make a pale blue. Cut out a 6cm circle for the plate underneath the birthday cake and a 3cm circle for the small plate beside the girl bear.

2. Place the spacers on the work surface with the grooves facing inwards and roll out 110g of Golden Bear Brown Sugar Dough. Cut out two 5cm circles then remove a slice from each circle. Fix the bottom layer of the cake on top of the plate then make the white filling from 5g of Sugar Dough. Roll the Sugar Dough into a ball and then flatten it with your fingers, keeping the edges rounded until it is the same size as the bottom layer of the cake. Again, remove a slice and stick the remaining filling to the cake. Repeat this

process with Red Sugar Dough for the strawberry jam and attach it to the white filling. Make another circle of white filling and secure this to the jam. Stick the top layer of the cake over the fillings and add a final coating of White Sugar Dough to the top.

3. Make a small slice of cake from the removed pieces for the teddy to hold. Use the small end of tool no. 11 to take a small piece out of the slice, as if it has been bitten.

4. Make an iced bun for the small teddy using Golden Bear Brown, White and Red Sugar Dough.

5. Roll 15g of White Sugar Dough into a long, thin sausage shape. Divide it into three sticks for the candles and cut a straight edge at each end. Push a piece of raw spaghetti through the centre of each candle, leaving a little showing at the base to push into the cake. Make the flames from a little White Sugar Dough mixed with Marigold Paste Food Colour. Paint a spiral design around each candle using Marigold Liquid Food Colour and allow to dry. Apply a little Gildesol onto the finished candles and then dust them with Magic Sparkle Dust.

6. Push a small ball of Red Sugar Dough over the spaghetti at the base of the candles and push them into the cake. Roll a few more small balls, mark with a cocktail stick, and add to the top of the cake for strawberries. Put one strawberry on the plate and dust the top of the cake with Magic Sparkle Dust. Prick the inside of the cake using two cocktail sticks together then make a few crumbs on the plate. Fix the completed cake to the plate and secure it to the top of the table with edible glue.

Standing Bear

1. Mix 5g of White Sugar Dough with a tiny piece of Red Sugar Dough to make a pale pink shade for the envelope. Cut out a small rectangle and paint 'Happy Birthday' in the centre. Set aside to dry.

2. Roll 25g of Golden Bear Brown Sugar Dough into a sausage shape. Turn up and flatten the rounded ends then cut the sausage in half to make two legs. Push a length of raw spaghetti down through the centre of each leg, leaving 3cm showing at the top. Roll 35g of Golden Bear Brown Sugar Dough into a cone shape for the body. Apply some edible glue around the top of the legs and slip the body over the pieces of spaghetti. Leave the legs and body to dry overnight if possible.

3. Add 5g of Blue Sugar Dough to 35g of White Sugar Dough to make a pale blue shade. Roll this out and cut two rectangles measuring 4cm x 5cm for the trouser legs. Make sure that the side seams join perfectly down the side of each leg before sticking these pieces to the bear. Place the front piece of the overalls in place and mark in-between the legs with tool no. 4. Run some stitch marks down the side seams then stick the back piece in position and trim it straight at the sides if necessary. Mark in-between the legs as before.

TIP Using Sugar Dough to make your models enables you to dress your figures right away if you are in a hurry to complete the cake. However, if possible you should leave them overnight as they will be slightly firmer and, therefore, easier to handle.

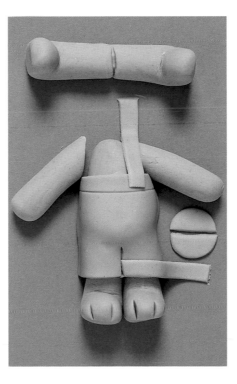

4. Cut out two small pockets using a 2cm circle cutter. Cut the circle in half and fix one pocket to the back and the other to the front of the bear's overalls. Roll out 5g of the pale blue Sugar Dough and cut out two strips for the turn-ups. Stick them around the lower edge of the trousers.

5. Roll 25g of Golden Bear Brown Sugar Dough into a sausage for the arms. Make a diagonal cut in the centre and attach them to the body. Cut two straps for the overalls and fix them in place, crossing them over at the back. Add two Red Sugar Dough buttons to the back of the overalls. Secure the envelope to the front of the body with some edible glue and position the paws at the edges.

6. Add a few coloured Sugar Dough patches to the bear and paint patterns on some of them with Liquid Food Colours.

7. Roll 25g of Golden Bear Brown Sugar Dough into a ball for the head. Apply some edible glue around the base and slip it over the spaghetti in the body. Remember to position the head so that the bear is looking downwards. Add the facial features, cheeks and ears.

Girl Teddy

1. Make the legs and body in the same way as previously described but position her sitting down on the cake top.

2. Roll out 30g of White Sugar Dough and cut out a 5cm circle for the petticoat. Use a cocktail stick to frill the edges then cut out a small circle in the centre. Place this over the body and arrange the frills. Mix 5g of Red Sugar Dough with 30g of White Sugar Dough to make the shade for the dress. Cut a 5cm circle for the skirt, remove a small circle in the centre, and slip this over the body on top of the petticoat. Apply some edible glue around the waistline and secure the skirt in position.

3. Roll out 25g of Golden Bear Brown into a sausage shape for the arms then make a diagonal cut in the centre. Stick them on either side of the body and fix the slice of cake in-between the paws. Place the small blue plate to the side of the bear and put a few cake crumbs on it. Add a small napkin by folding a square of White Sugar Dough in half.

4. Roll out 10g of White Sugar Dough and cut out two panels measuring 3cm x 2cm. Cut out a rounded neckline at the top of each panel using a small circle cutter. Roll out a very thin strip and cut it into six tiny lengths. Stick three pieces in a line across the both panels of the dress. Attach one panel to the front and one to the back of the body, covering the top edge of the skirt.

5. Roll out 5g of pink Sugar Dough into two strips. Make large frills in both strips to make the sleeves and secure them with edible glue to the top of the arms.

6. Roll 25g of Golden Bear Brown Sugar Dough into a ball for the head. Add the facial features, cheeks and ears and secure the finished head to the top of the body. Roll out 5g of pink Sugar Dough and cut out two small strips. Cut a 'V' shape out of the ends of the two strips and fix them onto the top of the head, one falling to the front and one to the back. Make the loops of the bow and fix in place. Secure the head in position, and then place the completed bear on the cake.

Small Teddy

Make a very small teddy from 30g of Golden Bear Brown Sugar Dough. Shape two small hearts from a tiny amount of Red Sugar Dough mixed with White Sugar Dough. Stick these to the paws of the teddy then position him in front of the table with the iced bun in his paws.

Bee Happy!

Children will love to help out with this cake, they will enjoy making the fun faces and could even make them look like their friends or party guests.

Materials

2 x 1 litre basin cakes

1.9kg (4lb 3oz) white sugarpaste

140g (5oz) SK Sugar Dough: Flesh

350g (12oz) SK Sugar Florist Paste (SFP): White

SK Paste Food Colours: Berberis, Blackberry, Bulrush, Sunflower and Teddy Bear Brown

SK Dust Food Colour: Berberis

SK Pastel Dust Food Colour: Pastel Pink

SK Edible Glue

❁

Equipment

20.5cm and 33cm (8" and 13") round cake drums

Non-stick board and rolling pin

SK Modelling Tools

SK Sugar Dough Press

SK Paintbrushes: nos. 0 and 10

Circle cutters: small (CT)

Heart cutter: 2cm (³/₄") (PME)

Leaf Cutter: 3.5cm (1³/₈") (PME)

Sunflower cutters: large and small (TT)

Tweezers

Flower pick

Floristry wire: gold

Flower formers

Covering the Cakes and Boards

1. Colour 1kg of sugarpaste with Berberis Paste Food Colour. Cover the two boards and attach the small one centrally on top of the larger one. Set aside to dry.

2. Using the remainder of the sugarpaste, cover the cakes in one and allow to dry. Position the cake in the centre of the board.

3. Colour 800g of sugarpaste, including any left over from covering the boards, with Teddy Bear Brown Paste Food Colour. Divide the cake into four sections from the top downwards by marking the sugarpaste covering lightly. Roll out a long sausage of the light brown sugarpaste and attach it to the cake. Ensure the paste is long enough to go around the circumference of the cake and position the join on one of the lines marked earlier. Secure the paste to the covered cake with edible glue. Continue with another sausage of paste, this time positioning the join at the next line on the cake. Repeat this process, ensuring that the joins follow on in sequence. Fill in the space at the top of the cake with a cone of paste.

4. Push a posy pick down into the centre of the cake. At this point, trim the cake drums with ribbon before you proceed with the decoration.

Sunflowers

1. Colour 350g of White SFP with Sunflower Paste Food Colour. Roll out the paste thinly and cut out one set of petals. Using tool no. 5 or a cocktail stick, roll each petal from side to side to widen and slightly curl the sides. Push tool no. 1 into some of the petals from the tip to the centre to give them some movement. Place the completed set of petals into a flower former.

2. Prepare a second layer of petals in exactly the same way and glue both layers together, making sure that the petals are staggered. Dust the base of the petals lightly with Berberis Dust Food Colour.

IMPORTANT NOTE Where wires are used on cakes, they should never be pushed straight into the cake as they may cause injury if eaten accidentally. Where wires are required, push a posy pick (see stockists) into the cake and fill with the same colour paste as the surrounding area to cover the top. The wire can then be pushed into this paste. It is important to ensure that the wire does not penetrate the cake. If the cake is to be given as a gift, remember to inform the recipient if there are wires in the cake before it is eaten.

3. Repeat the method to make five large and nine small sunflowers, each with two layers of petals.

4. To make the faces you will require 100g of Flesh Sugar Dough. For each face, roll 10g of paste into a small ball and flatten slightly with the palm of your hand to make a dome shape. Add a small ball for the nose in the centre of the face and secure with edible glue. Mark a smile just below the nose using tool no. 11. Make two small holes for the eyes, using tool no. 5 and fill in the eyes with the colour of your choice. Apply some edible glue to the back of the face and place the face into the centre of the flower.

5. To make the hair, add some white vegetable fat to a small ball of Sugar Dough in your chosen colour and extrude the paste through a Sugar Dough Press. (I have used Blackberry, Bulrush, Sunflower and Berberis Paste Food Colours.) Arrange the hair on the head and leave to dry completely.

6. Make the centres for the smaller sunflowers around the bottom of the

cake in exactly the same way from 40g of sugarpaste coloured with Bulrush Paste Food Colour. Divide the paste into five, roll each piece into a ball, flatten with the palm of your hand to make a dome shape, then take a pair of tweezers and pinch the top of the flower centre all over. Brush some edible glue on the back and secure it in position.

7. Arrange the five sunflowers evenly round the base of the cake, secure them in place with edible glue and fill the gaps with the smaller flowers.

Baby Sunflowers

Make four faces for the small sunflowers at the top of the cake and add a curl for the hair to make them look like babies. Arrange these around the top of the cake to hide the cone shape. You may need to support the flowers until they are dry.

Bees on the Hive

1. Roll out 15g of SFP coloured with Sunflower Paste Food Colour and cut out three bodies using a 3.5cm leaf cutter

and three heads using a 2cm circle cutter. Set aside.

2. Roll out some black-coloured SFP and cut some thin strips for the stripes on the body. Secure the stripes in place using edible glue. Roll two small feet and glue them underneath the body. Roll out a thin strip of the paste for the antennae, fold it into a 'V' shape and glue to the top of the head. Cut out three more 2cm circles in black, cut off a crescent shape at the top and glue one to the top of the head to cover the antennae.

3. Roll a tiny orange oval for the nose and glue to the centre of the face. Using a no. 0 paintbrush and some Blackberry Paste Food Colour, paint on the eyes and smile.

4. Cut out three hearts for the wings using a 2cm heart cutter and a little White SFP. Glue the wings to the body, then glue the completed head to the body and secure the three bees to the cake. Remember that two bees will be flying to the right and one to the left.

Bees on Wires

1. Make four more bees in the same way as before, but cut out an extra yellow body shape for each bee so that you can sandwich the wire in-between the two.

2. Cut a double length of gold floristry wire for each bee. Make some strong glue by adding a little pastillage powder to edible glue and mix it together to make a thick paste. Dab some glue on the back of each bee, place the wires on the top and place the second body shape. Press the two layers together and keep them flat until they have dried.

3. Push a piece of paste into the flower pick and insert the wires into this. Ensure the pick is removed before the cake is eaten.

Materials

15cm, 20.5cm and 25.5cm (6", 8" and 10") round cakes

2.6kg (5lb 12oz) white sugarpaste

SK Sugar Dough: 200g (7oz) Black, 140g (5oz) Brown, 150g (5¹/₄oz) Golden Bear Brown, 250g (9oz) White and 25g (1oz) Yellow

110g (3³/₄oz) SK Sugar Florist Paste (SFP): White

SK Paste Food Colours: Gentian and Poinsettia

SK Metallic Lustre Dust: Snowflake

SK Liquid Food Colour: Blackberry

SK Confectioners' Glaze

SK Edible Glue

Raw spaghetti

White vegetable fat

❀

Equipment

35.5cm (14") round cake drum

Non-stick board and rolling pin

SK Modelling Tools

SK Spacers and Sizing Cutters

SK Sugar Dough Press

SK Paintbrushes: nos. 0 and 10

Blossom plunger cutters (PME)

Circle cutters: small (CT)

Design wheel: (PME)

Bead maker: 6mm (CC)

Templates (see page 106)

Oh, Happy Day!

'Jumping the broom' is an African tradition dating back hundreds of years. The ritual symbolises the bride and groom's leap into married life and their commitment to each other.

Covering the Cakes and Board

1. To cover the board, colour 600g of white sugarpaste with Poinsettia Paste Food Colour. Cut out a 23cm circle out of the centre, leaving enough red paste to make the carpet down the cake.

2. Cover the three cakes using 2kg of white sugarpaste. Dowel the middle and base tiers (see page 9) and stack the cakes off the board. Roll out the remaining red sugarpaste and cut a strip measuring 46cm x 6cm to make the carpet. Check that this fits before you apply a line of edible glue all the way down the front of the cakes. To attach the red carpet, begin at the base of the large cake, working your way up to the top. Trim at the back of the top tier and at the base of the bottom tier. Offset the cakes on the board, leaving a 4cm space at the back.

3. Using the bead maker, make the beads to go around the cakes from 80g of White SFP. Dust the beads with Snowflake Metallic Lustre Dust and then secure each length to the base of the cake with edible glue, joining them together neatly.

Groom

1. Roll two small ovals of Black Sugar Dough for the shoes, mark the sole using tool no. 8 and make stitch marks at the front using tool no. 12.

2. To make the legs, roll 40g of Black Sugar Dough into a sausage shape, cut in half and make a straight cut at the top and bottom. Hollow out the base of the trousers to fit over the shoes and pinch a crease in the trousers by gently squeezing the paste with your finger and thumb. Stand each leg over the top of the shoe and push a piece of dry spaghetti down through the centre and into the shoe. Glue a thin, black strip down the side of each trouser leg.

3. Roll 20g of Black Sugar Dough into a cone shape for the body. Apply some edible glue to the top of the legs and slip the body over the spaghetti.

4. Roll out a small piece of grey Sugar Dough and cut out the waistcoat using the template. Mark a diagonal stitch pattern using tool no. 12 and secure the waistcoat to the front of the body. Add a tie made from Black Sugar Dough. Dust the waistcoat and tie with Snowflake Metallic Lustre Dust.

5. Roll out 40g of Black Sugar Dough and cut out the two halves of the jacket, using the template as a guide. Secure the jacket from the front to the back and adjust where necessary so that the seam fits neatly at the back. Roll out the remainder of the black paste, cut out the lapels using the template and attach them to the front of the jacket.

6. Roll a sausage of Black Sugar Dough for the sleeves, make a diagonal cut in the centre and a straight cut at each end, and push a small piece of raw

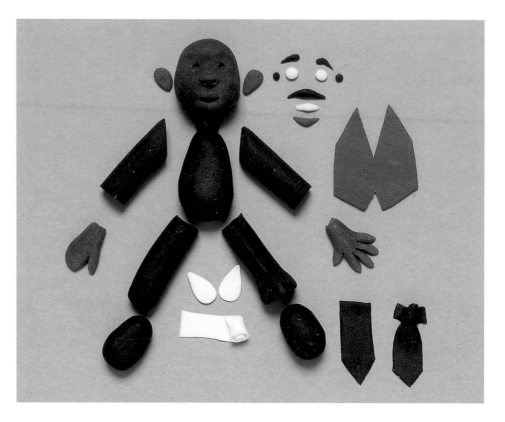

spaghetti into the end. Roll two hands from Brown Sugar Dough, cut out a 'V' shape to define the thumb, and then slightly flatten the rounded end. Mark four fingers using tool no. 4 and round off the edges on each finger. Attach the hands to the end of the sleeves and glue a small, white strip around the wrist. Attach the left arm only to the body and set the right arm aside until required.

7. Make the groom's head by rolling 20g of Brown Sugar Dough into a ball. Pull the neck out at the base and indent the eye area. Roll a small cone for the nose and mark the nostrils using tool no. 5. Mark the mouth using tool no. 11 and straighten the top lip by inserting using tool no. 10 into the mouth. Make a small, white banana shape for the teeth, make another banana shape for the lower lip and secure with edible glue. Add a small moustache under the nose and mark the centre with tool no. 4. Make two small teardrop shapes for the ears, attach to each

side of the head and indent with the end of a paintbrush. Roll two small, white balls for the eyes, secure in place, and then add the pupils. Finally, add small, black eyebrows.

8. Soften some Black Sugar Dough with white vegetable fat and fill the Sugar Dough Press. Squeeze out the shortest possible strands and cut off with tool no. 4. Brush the head with edible glue and arrange the hair on top of the head.

9. To make the groom's buttonhole, roll up a tiny strip of White Sugar Dough to make a small rose and twist the end to secure. Make three small leaves by rolling tiny cone shapes, flatten and mark with tool no. 5. Arrange the leaves around the rose and attach to the lapel.

Bride

1. Mix 45g of Brown Sugar Dough with 45g of Golden Bear Brown to make the flesh colour for the body. Make a tall cone shape and pull out the neck at the widest end. Shape the shoulders with your fingers and pull out the bust. Smooth and mould the body into a natural shape. The body should be 10cm high to the top of the neck. Push a piece of dry spaghetti down through the body, leaving 3cm showing at the neck.

> **TIP** If you find it too difficult to mould the body with the bust in one piece, then make the bust using two round balls secured with edible glue. Rub a little white vegetable fat into your hands for easier shaping.

2. Roll a ball from 5g of paste and taper at both ends, secure this across the stomach area, and then roll two balls for her bottom and secure in place.

3. Make two cone-shaped shoes from White Sugar Dough. The shoes should be slightly larger than normal to give the body a good base to stand on. Push a piece of raw spaghetti into the shoes, apply a little edible glue around the top and slip the shoes underneath the body. Set aside to dry. (As the bride is wearing a long gown, there is no need to make the legs separately.)

4. To make the skirt, roll out 35g of White Sugar Dough and cut out a strip measuring 13cm x 7cm. Adjust the width or length if necessary to fit around the body. Apply some edible glue around the waist area and attach the strip from the front to the back. Arrange the seam neatly at the back and leave a kick pleat at the bottom.

5. Using the template, cut out two pieces for the bodice from White Sugar Dough; again, adjust the size if necessary. Fit each piece from the front to the back (straight edge at the back) and join the front seam neatly. The back has a deep 'V' to the waist with thin laces joining the two pieces together.

6. To make the decoration on the right side of the dress, cut four ribbons of varying lengths from White Sugar Dough. Cut another strip measuring 1cm x 4cm, make four loops in the centre and squeeze together gently. Glue the ribbons at the waist and add the looped piece over the top. Open the loops with the end of a paintbrush.

7. Roll a ball for the head from 20g of Sugar Dough. Do not pull the neck down for the bride, but model the face as described for the groom. Make her features more feminine by making her eyes larger and giving her full lips. Outline the eyes with a no. 0 brush and Blackberry Liquid Food Colour.

8. Brush edible glue onto the head. To make the hair, soften 15g of Black Sugar Dough with white vegetable fat, extrude the hair through a Sugar Dough Press and shake to separate the strands. Lay the strands down on the work surface and arrange the hair in the style of your choice, working on just a few strands at a time.

9. To make the upper arms, roll a sausage of paste and then make a diagonal cut in the centre and a straight cut at each end. For the gloves, roll 10g of White Sugar Dough into a sausage shape, make a straight cut in the centre and slightly flatten the rounded end. Make the hands as described for the groom. Push a small piece of raw spaghetti into the top of each glove and attach to the upper arm with edible glue. Attach the right arm only, bringing the hand forward and gluing it to the front of the body.

10. Secure the bride to the top of the cake and stand the groom

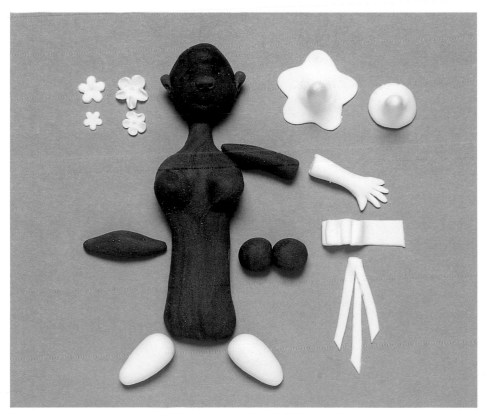

beside her in the required position, keeping them close together. Glue the groom's right arm into position at the shoulder, bringing his hand to rest on her bottom. Glue the bride's left arm to her shoulder and rest her hand on his shoulder. Leave in this position to dry. Make a choker from a thin strip of White Sugar Dough, join at the front and cover the join with a small cone.

11. Thinly roll 25g of White SFP into an irregular rectangular shape measuring 20cm long. Gather the veil neatly at the top and turn it under. Secure the veil to the top of the head with edible glue. Arrange the rest of the veil over the edge of the top tier but do not hide the back of the dress.

12. Make 30 small blossoms from thinly rolled White Sugar Dough using a blossom plunger cutter. Roll the edges of each petal using tool no. 5 and glue them around the edges and back of the veil. Attach three on the head, one on each ear lobe and one on the front of each shoe.

13. To make the posy, make a Mexican hat shape from 5g of White Sugar Dough. Using tool no. 5, roll out five petal shapes around the edge, and then glue a small ball of White Sugar Dough in the centre of the posy. Cut out 12 large blossoms and 12 small blossoms and frill the edges using tool no. 5. Glue the small petals on top of the large ones and arrange the flowers around the edge of the posy, working your way to the top. Cut and twist two thin ribbons, arrange on the side of the cake and glue the posy on top.

Pointing Girl

1. Mix together equal quantities of Yellow and White Sugar Dough to make a pale yellow colour. Roll 15g of this paste into a small cone shape for the body, place this on the middle tier and push a

piece of raw spaghetti down through the centre to hold it in place.

2. Mix equal quantities of Brown and Golden Bear Brown Sugar Dough to make the flesh colour, in the same way as for the bride. Roll 10g of this paste into a sausage shape, make a diagonal cut in the centre and a straight cut at each end. Push a small piece of raw spaghetti into the straight end. Roll 10g of White Sugar Dough into a small sausage shape for the lower leg (sock), cut it in half and turn up the rounded ends. Slice off the bottom of the feet. Attach the socks to the upper legs. Roll out a small strip of White Sugar Dough, run a design wheel along the paste and pull apart to make a picot edge. Glue a strip around the top of each sock.

3. Divide 5g of Black Sugar Dough equally and roll two oval shapes for

the shoes, mark the heel on each using tool no. 4 and attach to the foot. Cut a thin strip in black and glue this over the foot.

4. Roll out 15g of White Sugar Dough and cut two strips for the petticoat, long enough to be gathered and go around the body. Add the pale yellow skirt on the top and arrange the folds evenly.

5. Roll two small balls of pale yellow Sugar Dough for the sleeves. Make the arms and hands using the flesh-coloured Sugar Dough as previously described and arrange the fingers in a pointing position as shown. Attach the arms to the sleeves, push a small piece of spaghetti into the shoulder area and slip the sleeves into position.

6. Roll a ball for the head and pull out the neck area. Indent the eyes and add the nose, make the mouth by inserting the end of a paintbrush, and then complete the facial features as previously described.

7. Soften 15g of Black Sugar Dough. Place a thin layer of pale yellow Sugar Dough into the bottom of the Sugar Dough Press and fill the cup up with the black paste. Squeeze out the strands and layer them around the head. Add a small yellow bow to finish.

Book

Roll out 10g of Black Sugar Dough and cut out a 6cm x 4cm rectangle for the cover. Make the pages individually from White Sugar Dough by cutting out several rectangles measuring 3cm x 2cm. Stack them up on one side of the cover, adding a little glue in-between the pages, and fold the other side of the cover over. Mark the spine of the book with tool no. 4. Secure the book to the bottom tier of the cake.

Boy

1. Mix 25g of Golden Bear Brown Sugar Dough with an equal amount of White to make a light brown shade. Roll 20g of this paste into a cone shape for the body. Mix 20g of Brown Sugar Dough with the same amount of Golden Bear Brown to make the flesh colour, then use 15g of this paste to make the legs. Bend one leg slightly at the knee. Slice off the underside of each foot, as for the pointing girl.

2. Make the shoes in the same way as before from the light brown paste, attach to the foot and make a 'T' shaped strap to go over the front. Push a piece of raw spaghetti through the centre of each leg and into the shoe. Attach the legs to the body.

TIP Assemble the body and limbs flat on the work surface and hold it up against the side of the cake before securing in position with edible glue.

3. Make the jacket and trousers from the light brown Sugar Dough, using the templates as a guide. Attach the trousers first and trim at the sides if necessary, and then at the top. Make stitch marks down the back and add two small pockets. Next, attach the top loosely around the lower edge and tuck in the paste around the sides. Secure the figure to the cake at this point and support the bent leg with foam until dry.

4. To make the sleeves, roll a sausage of light brown paste and make a diagonal cut in the centre. Hollow out the inside slightly using tool no. 1. Secure the sleeves to the body on the side of the cake.

5. Using the flesh-coloured Sugar Dough, make two arms as described for the pointing girl and attach to the sleeves. Bend both arms at the elbow and position them on top of the top tier.

6. Using the template as a guide, cut out the collar and add stitch marks around the edge. Attach to the top of the body.

7. Roll 15g of the flesh-coloured Sugar Dough into a ball for the head and add the facial features as previously described (a neck is not required). Glue the head to the top of the body, turning it to look to the right. Extrude a few strands of hair using 5g of Black Sugar Dough and glue to the top of the head.

Singing Girl

1. Colour 25g of White Sugar Dough with Gentian Paste Food Colour for the dress. Roll 15g of the blue paste into a cone shape for the body and position on the edge of the base tier. Insert a piece of raw spaghetti through the middle, leaving 3cm showing at the top.

2. Blend 20g of Brown Sugar Dough with the same amount of Golden Bear Brown for the flesh colour. Roll out 15g of this paste for the legs, shaping them as before.

3. Roll two small oval shapes of White Sugar Dough for the shoes and secure to the legs with a short piece of raw spaghetti. Roll a thin strip of White Sugar Dough for the sock top and attach around the ankle, rolling over the paste at the top. Make a small bow for the front of each shoe.

4. Make a white petticoat in the same way as for the other girl. For the skirt, roll out some of the blue paste and cut out a 5cm circle. Cut out a smaller circle from the centre and slip this over the body, arranging the skirt over the petticoat.

5. Make the waistcoat, using the template as a guide. Secure the waistcoat to the front of the dress.

6. Make the arms and hands as previously described and secure to the shoulders. Apply some edible glue to the palms of the hands and bring them together at the front. Support with foam until dry. Make a small, blue frill for the sleeve and attach over the top.

7. Make the head in the same way as for the pointing girl, but this time pull down the mouth with the end of a paintbrush. Add two small pieces of White Sugar Dough for the teeth. Outline the eyes with a no. 0 paintbrush and some Blackberry Liquid Food Colour.

8. Brush the head with edible glue. Roll several long, thin strands of Black Sugar Dough and twist them together to make the braids. Arrange them side-by-side on either side of the parting and add some coloured balls of Sugar Dough for the beads.

Broom

1. Break a piece of raw spaghetti to the length of the broom. Soften 10g of Golden Bear Brown Sugar Dough and fill the cup of the Sugar Dough Press. Extrude strands long enough for the broom handle and cover the raw spaghetti. Make the bristles by extruding and cutting off shorter strands and attaching them to the handle. Make single strands to bind the handle together.

2. Make some ribbons and flowers from White Sugar Dough to dress the broom and dust with Snowflake Metallic Lustre Dust. Attach to the front of the board.

Finishing Touches

Add some small beads around the children's wrists and around the top of the bride's gloves, and give her a wedding ring. Highlight the shoes, book, hair and bride's lips with confectioners' glaze.

If the Shoe Fits ...Buy It!

Decisions, decisions, so difficult to make, especially where shoes are concerned!

Materials

10cm x 15.5cm and 20.5cm x 25.5cm (4" x 6" and 8" x 10") oval cakes

1.4kg (3lb 1oz) white sugarpaste

SK Sugar Dough: 45g ($1^1/_2$oz) Black, 10g ($^1/_3$oz) Blue, 10g ($^1/_3$oz) Brown, 100g ($3^1/_2$oz) Flesh, 50g ($1^3/_4$oz) Golden Bear Brown, 20g ($^3/_4$oz) Green, 10g ($^1/_3$oz) Red, 10g ($^1/_3$oz) Violet, 300g ($10^1/_2$oz) White and 10g ($^1/_3$oz) Yellow

SK Paste Food Colour: Rose

SK Designer Paste Food Colour: Bordeaux

SK Pastel Dust Colour: Pastel Pink

SK Magic Sparkle Dust

SK Liquid Food Colours: Bluebell, Bulrush, Daffodil, Mint and Poinsettia

SK Confectioners' Glaze

SK Edible Glue

❀

Equipment

28cm x 33cm (11" x 13") oval cake drum

Non-stick board and rolling pin

SK Modelling Tools

SK Paintbrushes: nos. 0 and 2

Circle cutters: small (CT)

Rectangle cutters: small (CT)

Alphabet script cutters (FMM)

Template (see page 107)

Covering the Cakes and Board

1. Carve out one side of the small cake to create a crescent shape, using the template as a guide. Colour 600g of sugarpaste with Bordeaux Paste Food Colour, cover the board and set aside to dry. Colour the trimmings (approximately 200g) a deeper shade of Bordeaux and cover the small cake. Colour 800g of sugarpaste with Rose Paste Food Colour and cover the large oval cake.

2. Offset the large cake on the board and position the small cake (the seat) at the back of the larger one. Dust the seat with Magic Sparkle Dust.

Shoe Boxes

1. To make the large open box, roll out some White Sugar Dough and cut out a rectangle for the base measuring 4cm x 2.5cm, or you can use the large cutter from the set. For the sides, cut out a strip measuring 14cm x 1.5cm. Run a line of edible glue along one edge and attach the strip around the oblong shape. Finish with a neat join at one corner. Set aside to dry. Make the tissue paper from a small, thin piece of White Sugar Dough. Make the lid in the same way as the box and trim with a narrower strip around the edge. Make four open boxes and one lid.

2. Make four large, closed boxes by rolling out 80g of White Sugar Dough between the spacers, giving a thickness of 1cm. Use this for the base of each box. Roll out a thin strip of paste for each one and glue this around the top of the box, joining neatly at the corner, to create the lid.

TIP I have made the shoe boxes from White Sugar Dough and then painted them various colours. However, if you have leftover pieces of coloured paste from other projects, you can use them up.

3. Follow the same instructions to make three small boxes, measuring 3cm x 2cm.

4. Paint the boxes bright colours using various Liquid Food Colours and set aside to dry.

Shoes

1. **Boots:** roll two small, red sausage shapes, curve them into an 'L' shape and make a straight cut at the top. Using tool no. 1, hollow out the tops and make stitch marks. Make the soles from Brown Sugar Dough, secure with edible glue and mark the heel using tool no. 4.

2. **Flip flops:** make soles in different colours and place one on top of the other. Press down the foot area and lift the heel, and then place a twisted strap over the front.

3. **Sandals:** make three soles and stack them up. Add straps around the foot and ankle.

4. **Loafers:** roll two small sausage shapes, hollow out the top using tool no. 1 and add a sole.

5. **Court shoes:** roll two small sausage shapes, pull down the heel from underneath and shape with your fingers. Place the shoe on top of tool no. 4 and mould the shoe around the tool to give a high instep.

Dog

1. To make the basket, cut out a base using the large oblong cutter, cut out a strip for the sides measuring 14cm x 2cm and glue this around the base. When dry, paint on a check design using a no. 0 paintbrush and some Bulrush Liquid Food Colour mixed with a little Daffodil. Cut out two small circles for the handles and secure with edible glue.

2. Make the dog from Golden Bear Brown Sugar Dough. Start by rolling a cone shape for the body and gently pull out the tail to a point from the thickest end. Roll two small cones for the back legs, bend into position and attach to the dog. Place the dog inside the basket.

3. Push a short piece of raw spaghetti into the top of the body to support the head. Roll a cone shape for the head and flatten the front to form a snout. Brush the base with edible glue and push the head over the spaghetti. Mark the centre of the face with a line, and then add a small smile on either side using tool no. 11. Make a small hole for the mouth and insert a tiny

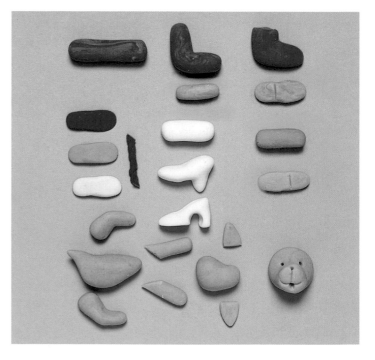

If The Shoe Fits

pink tongue. Add a small black cone for the nose. Using tool no. 5, make two small holes for the eyes and fill with tiny balls of Brown Sugar Dough. Roll two small sausage shapes for the front paws, divide in the centre and attach to the dog. Make two small cone shapes for the ears, flatten them with your fingers, make a straight cut at the widest end and attach to the head. Paint the tail with Bulrush Liquid Food Colour using a no. 0 paintbrush.

Girl

1. Blend 60g of Flesh Sugar Dough with 20g of Golden Bear Brown to make the flesh colour. Use 20g of this paste to roll a tall cone shape for the body and add a tummy button using tool no. 5.

2. For the skirt, mix 10g of White Sugar Dough with 5g of Yellow to make a lemon shade. Roll out 10g of this paste into a strip and cut it to measure 6cm x 2cm,

making the long sides slightly curved, as shown. Place this around and underneath the body at the back, so that the girl is sitting on the skirt, and bring it around the sides.

3. Make the sandals using Blue and White Sugar Dough as previously described.

4. For the legs, roll 20g of the flesh-coloured paste into a sausage shape and make a diagonal cut in the centre. Roll the paste slightly narrower at the ankles and back of the knees to make the legs more shapely, then make a diagonal cut at the back of each foot and secure the sandals in place. Cross one leg over the other.

5. Cut out the front of the skirt using the remaining lemon-coloured paste and secure at each side of the body.

6. Mix equal quantities of Green and White Sugar Dough to make a pale

green colour for the crop top. Roll out and cut a rectangle measuring 8cm x 2cm. Cut out a semi-circle from the edge to create the neckline. Apply some edible glue around the upper body and wrap the strip around the body, making a neat join at the back. Ease the paste in at the shoulders.

7. Roll a ball from 20g of the flesh-coloured paste for the head. Pull out the neck and indent the eye area, nose and ears. Push the end of a paintbrush into the mouth. Add two small, white balls for the eyes and small, black pupils looking upwards to give her an air of indecision. Outline the eyes using Bulrush Liquid Food Colour and a no. 0 paintbrush. Add two small eyebrows and outline the mouth with Poinsettia Liquid Food Colour. Make two small teardrop shapes for the ears and indent with the end of a paintbrush.

8. Roll a sausage shape from 20g of flesh-coloured paste for the arms and make a diagonal cut in the centre. Cut

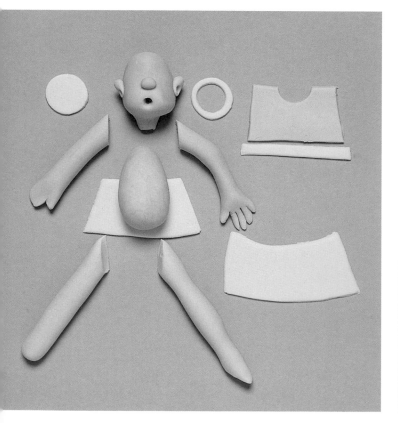

out a 'V' shape to make the thumb and divide the four fingers. Soften the edges and lengthen the fingers. Attach the arms to the body and rest the right arm over a stack of shoe boxes. Apply edible glue to the palm of the left hand and place it over the mouth.

9. Make two yellow earrings using two of the small, round cutters and glue them onto the ears when dry.

Shop Assistant

1. Soften 40g of Black Sugar Dough with a little white vegetable fat, and then roll into a large cone shape. Make a slit in the widest end for the legs, and roll the edges until they are smooth. Make a straight cut at the bottom of each leg. Bend at the knee and sit the body on the legs in a kneeling position. Push a piece of raw spaghetti through the body, leaving 3cm showing at the neck.

2. Mix some Black and White Sugar Dough together to make grey and roll two small oval shapes for the shoes. Add a small brown sole as previously described and attach the completed shoes to the end of each leg, turning the toes inwards.

3. To make the t-shirt, roll out 20g of White Sugar Dough and cut out two 5cm squares. Make a diagonal cut at the sleeve seams, and then attach the back and front of the shirt to the body, making a neat seam at the side. Add a small strip to the front where the t-shirt will button up and indent the buttons with a piece of raw spaghetti.

4. Model the head as before using 20g of Flesh Sugar Dough. Indent the eyelids lightly using tool no. 11 and outline the eyes using a fine paintbrush and Bulrush Liquid Food Colour. Slip the head over the spaghetti and secure in place with edible glue. Roll a small strip of White Sugar Dough for the collar, making it long enough to go around the neck, and secure in place.

5. Make the arms as described for the girl from Flesh Sugar Dough. Cut two small strips for the sleeves and wrap them around the top of the arms. Make a diagonal cut at the top and bend at the elbows.

6. Place the boxes and shoes in front of the figure and secure to the cake. Rest one arm on the shoes with other holding the head.

7. Soften 10g of Brown Sugar Dough with white vegetable fat and shape the paste around the head like a cap. Mark the hair using tool no. 4.

8. Thinly roll out 10g of White SFP and cut out the letters to go around the cake using the alphabet script cutters. Use edible glue to secure the letters to the cake.

Finishing Touches

Dust the cheeks of both figures with Pastel Pink Dust Food Colour. Highlight the eyes and shoes with confectioners' glaze. Arrange the remaining shoes and boxes on top of the cake and secure in place with edible glue.

Materials

25.5cm (10") hexagonal cake

1.2kg (2lb 10oz) white sugarpaste

SK Sugar Dough: 30g (1oz) Black, 70g (2$^1/_2$oz) Blue, 30g (1oz) Brown, 185g (6$^1/_2$oz) Flesh, 170g (6oz) Golden Bear Brown, 115g (4oz) Green, 50g (1$^1/_2$oz) Orange, 145g (5oz) Red, 50g (1$^1/_2$oz) Violet, 470g White and 15g ($^1/_2$oz) Yellow

SK Sugar Florist Paste (SFP): 40g (1$^1/_4$oz) White

SK Paste Food Colours: Daffodil, Gentian and Marigold

SK Dust Food Colours: Bluebell, Edelweiss and Marigold

SK Moon Beams Lustre Dusts: Sapphire and Topaz

SK Pastel Dust Food Colour: Pastel Pink

SK Liquid Food Colours: Bluebell, Bulrush, Gentian, Marigold, Mint and Poinsettia

SK Instant Mix Pastillage (small amount)

SK Edible Glue

Raw spaghetti

White vegetable fat

❀

Equipment

33cm (13") hexagonal cake drum

Non-stick board and rolling pin

SK Modelling Tools

SK Spacers and Sizing Cutters

SK Sugar Dough Press

SK Paintbrushes: nos. 0, 2 and 10

Circle cutters: small (CT)

Design wheel (PME)

Rectangle cutters: small (CT)

Rice textured rolling pin (CC)

Floristry wire: gold

Fine sandpaper (new)

Cocktail stick

Floppy mat (SC)

School Days

This familiar scene can be made on a cake to give to your child's favourite teacher or to raise funds at a school fair. You can personalise the cake by making each child look like your own children and their friends or by writing the names of the class members on the pictures.

Covering the Cake and Board

1. Colour 1kg of sugarpaste with Daffodil Paste Food Colour. Use 200g of this to cover the board and set the rest aside to cover the cake. Roll out a strip of the yellow sugarpaste measuring 4cm x 23cm then use the rice patterned rolling pin to texture the surface. Lay this piece along one section of the board and then roll a second strip of the same size and place it along the edge of the following section where it will overlap the previous one. Cut diagonally through the two layers then carefully remove the piece underneath and the overlapping piece on top to make a mitred join. Repeat this step to cover the rest of the board.

2. Roll out the remaining sugarpaste and cover the cake. Fix the cake to the centre of the board.

Side Designs

1. **Crayons:** make 18 crayons in total, using 15g of White Sugar Dough for each one. Shape each crayon by rolling the Sugar Dough into a sausage shape, make a straight cut at one end and roll a point at the other end. Push a small round cutter over the pointed end to make a ridge around the end of the crayon. Wrap thinly-rolled SFP in different colours around the top and bottom of each one and add two thin strips of Black SFP for the label. Secure the finished crayons to two sides of the cake using edible glue.

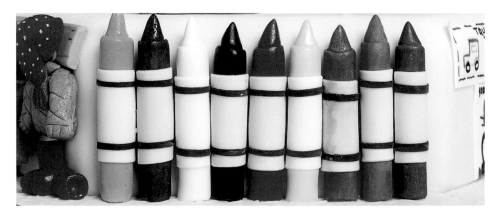

2. **Children's pictures:** roll out 20g of White SFP very thinly and cut out five rectangles, three for one side of the cake and two for the other. Curl up some of the corners then paint a child-like picture and a name on each one using Liquid Food Colours. Allow to dry and then secure in place.

3. **Cloakroom pegs:** roll 50g of Golden Bear Brown Sugar Dough into two strips measuring 14cm x 2cm for the peg rail. Paint on the wood effect using a fine paintbrush and Bulrush Liquid Food Colour. Push four small pieces of raw spaghetti into each strip, spacing them out evenly. Make the pegs from eight small sausage shapes moulded into 'S' shapes, leaving one end longer than the other. Apply edible glue to the short end and push it over the raw spaghetti in the rail. Once dry, attach the peg rails to the sides of the cake using strong sugar glue (pastillage powder mixed with edible glue).

Clothes in the Cloakroom

1. For the first peg (at the back of the cake), make the little school satchel from 15g of Golden Bear Brown Sugar Dough as shown. The flap is made using a 2.5cm circle cutter with $1/3$ of the circle removed. Model a blue coat and cap from 30g of White Sugar Dough coloured with

Gentian Paste Food Colour. Outline the peak of the cap with SK Bluebell Liquid Food Colour. Once the peg is completely dry, hang the satchel over the peg, indent the underside of the cap and secure it to the cake and on the peg with strong sugar glue (you may need to support it with foam until dry) and place the jacket into position on the board, securing with edible glue.

2. To make a coat for the second peg, cut a 5cm square from Green Sugar Dough, fold the top corners under to make a triangular shape and then make a fold down the centre. Secure to the side of the

cake, directly under the second peg. Roll out the two sleeves as before and stick these over the coat then cut out a 4cm circle for the hood and gather this at the top. Attach the hood to the top of the coat. Make a small white bag and use a design wheel to add a pattern. Hang the bag over the peg and secure with edible glue. Model a pair of green boots and secure them to the board.

3. Make a coat and scarf from 30g of Red Sugar Dough for the next peg. Make the coat in the same way as before, but this time, turn the lower edge under to

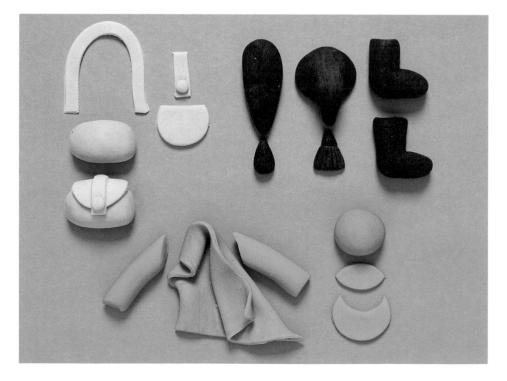

shorten it. Stick this piece to the side of the cake and then attach the sleeves and collar. Cut a strip of paste for the scarf, make a fringe at the ends and paint on the stripes using diluted Edelweiss Dust Food Colour. Pinch the scarf at the centre and secure in place on the peg.

4. Take 25g of Violet Sugar Dough and make the coat as before. Add a small belt at the back then attach it to the peg. Support it with foam until dry. Add white piping around the collar and cuffs from a tiny strip of White Sugar Dough and use tool no. 12 to create a fur effect.

5. For the left-hand peg at the front of the cake, make a scarf from 15g of Green Sugar Dough, cut a fringe at each end and add two square pockets. Mark them with stitch marks using tool no. 12 then pinch the scarf in the centre and attach it to the peg.

6. Mix together 25g of White Sugar Dough and 5g of Violet Sugar Dough, cut out a rectangle measuring approximately 5cm x 6cm and make the coat as before. Cut out a circle for the hood using a 2.5cm circle cutter, gather slightly and turn up the edges then secure to the top of the coat with edible glue. Dust the coat all over with Topaz Moon Beams Lustre Dust.

7. Cut out a 5cm square from 25g of Orange Sugar Dough then make the coat as before. Add a collar and belt, then paint a line around the collar and two small buttons on the sleeve with Bulrush Liquid Food Colour. To make the hat, cut out a 1.5cm circle from 5g of Brown Sugar Dough and stick a small ball of Brown Sugar Dough in the middle. Add an orange ribbon, then make a thin brown loop to go over the peg and attach the hat to the coat and the loop.

8. Mix 20g of White Sugar Dough with 5g of Blue and use 10g of the

mixture to model a soft, triangular shape. Use tool no. 4 to mark the coat with a criss-cross design. Roll the sleeves and mark them in the same way, adding a ribbed pattern at the cuffs. Stick the coat to the cake, directly underneath the peg, and then add the sleeves. Roll a small sausage shape for the collar and secure in place. Roll a cone from 10g of Red Sugar Dough for the hat, bend the point down and add a small tassel on the end. Paint on the dots using diluted Edelweiss Dust Food Colour. Secure the hat to the peg with edible glue. Make the boots from 10g of Red Sugar Dough and secure to the board.

Teacher

1. To make the stool for the teacher, roll a piece of pastillage between two spacers to keep it level. Cut out two 4.5cm squares for the sides of the stool and use a 2.5cm circle cutter to remove a circular shape from the base of the squares. Cut out a 5cm square for the seat of the stool then leave all the pieces to dry out on a flat surface overnight. Once the pieces are dry, rub down any rough edges with fine sandpaper then assemble the stool upside-down, using strong sugar glue to secure. Leave in this position until the glue has set, then paint the stool with Bulrush Liquid Food Colour and set aside to dry.

2. Roll out 5g of Blue Sugar Dough and cut out the book cover using the 3cm rectangle cutter. Roll out 5g of White Sugar Dough very thinly and cut out the pages using the same oblong cutter, then trim them slightly smaller than the cover. Place the pages loosely on top of each other, securing in place with edible glue in the centre of the book. Fold the book in half and mark the spine with tool no. 4. Open it out and shape the pages to make them slightly arched. Set the book aside to dry.

3. Model an apple from Red Sugar Dough then make a small hole at the top and in the side. Dab a little edible glue into both holes and insert a tiny stalk at the top of the apple and a worm in the side. Paint on two dots for the worm's eyes then dust the apple with Marigold Dust Food Colour. Secure it to the stool after you have made the teacher.

4. Roll 20g of Flesh Sugar Dough into a cone shape for the teacher's body then shape the neck, shoulders, waistline, hips and bust. Once you have the basic shape of the figure, make a straight cut straight at the base. Apply some edible glue to the base of the body, stick it in the centre of the stool, then push a piece of raw spaghetti through the neck to support the head later.

5. Roll 20g of Flesh Sugar Dough into a sausage shape, cut it in half for the legs and shape the ankle and knees. Bend the legs at the knee and make a diagonal cut at the top and under the foot.

6. For the shoes, roll two small ovals from Black Sugar Dough. Press out the sole and heel between your finger and thumb then fix the soles to the underside of the feet, bringing them up slightly at the back of the heel. Roll another tiny oval shape, flatten it and place it over the toe area, then trim to fit if necessary. Repeat for the other foot. Roll out two tiny straps and secure them over the feet. Once the shoes are in place, stick the legs to the front of the body.

7. Roll out 25g of Golden Bear Brown Sugar Dough and cut an oval shape measuring approximately 12cm x 4cm (at the widest part). Fold this over and tuck in the edges. Loosely wrap it around the body as the back of the skirt, bringing it around to the front and resting it on the stool, close to the side of the legs. Cut out a rectangle measuring 9cm x 6cm for the front of the skirt, turn the side edges under and arrange it to fit the body. Cut a thin strip to go down the front of the skirt and add stitch marks with a design wheel or tool no. 12. Add some tiny Red Sugar Dough buttons to finish the skirt.

8. Cut out two rectangles from Red Sugar Dough, both measuring 6cm x 4cm, for the jumper. You may need to trim these pieces to fit neatly on the body. Make sure that the seams sit neatly down the sides the cut out a little at the neck area using a small circle cutter. Make stitch marks along the welt at the bottom using tool no. 12. Secure the jumper to the body with edible glue. To neaten the neckline, roll out a thin piece of Red Sugar Dough, cut out a 2cm circle then take out the centre with a 1.5cm circle cutter. Brush with edible glue and slip this over the spaghetti at the neck. Make two small balls of Red Sugar Dough for the sleeves. Push a piece of raw spaghetti into each shoulder and secure the sleeves in place. Mark the creases in the fabric with tool no. 4. Push a small piece of raw spaghetti into each sleeve to support the arms later.

9. Make the arms from 10g of Flesh Sugar Dough. Bend them at the elbow and flatten the hand slightly. Cut a straight edge just above the elbow. Shape the fingers and mark the nails with the end of a piece of raw spaghetti. Paint the nails with Poinsettia Liquid Food Colour and allow them to dry. Apply edible glue to the arm and slip it over the spaghetti in the sleeve. Position the book in the hands,

secure with edible glue and support it with a little foam until dry.

10. Roll 20g of Flesh Sugar Dough into a smooth, round ball for the head. Make a slight indentation for the eyes then add a small oval shape for the nose. Use tool no. 11 to gently mark the shape of the eyelid. Stick two small cone shapes on for the ears and push the end of a paintbrush into the bottom of the ears to make a small hole, securing them firmly to the head. Add two earrings then mark the mouth with a smile using tool no. 11. Straighten the top lip slightly by inserting tool no. 2.

11. Using a no. 0 paintbrush and a mixture of Bulrush and Marigold Liquid Food Colours, paint on the eyelashes, eyebrows and eyelids. Paint the lips with Poinsettia Liquid Food Colour. Dust the eyelids with Bluebell Dust Food Colour and the cheeks with Pastel Pink. Apply a little edible glue to the neck and slip the head over the top, tilting it forward slightly. Allow to dry.

12. Soften 25g of Golden Bear Brown Sugar Dough with some white vegetable fat and extrude strands of hair through the Sugar Dough Press. When they are about 5cm long, use a cocktail stick to remove several strands in a row, make a straight cut at the top of the strands and begin to layer the hair on the head. Once you have made the parting and covered the head, make some ringlets by twisting two or three short strands together. Cut out three small circles form Red Sugar Dough, fold them in half and in half again to form the hair decoration. Apply some edible glue to the back and then push a cocktail stick into the centre of the decoration and push this into the hair.

13. Position the figure and stool on the cake, using some strong sugar glue on the base of each stool leg to fix it in place.

for the mouth. Roll two tiny balls of White Sugar Dough for the eyes and stick them in place. Add the pupils then use Bulrush Liquid Food Colour to outline the eyes, eyelashes and eyebrows. Dust the cheeks with Pastel Pink Dust Food Colour then push the completed head over the spaghetti at the neck, securing it with edible glue.

7. Cut out a 2cm circle from White Sugar Dough to make a small collar. Cut the circle in half and secure to the dress on either side of the neck.

8. Soften 10g of Brown Sugar Dough with white vegetable fat and fill the Sugar Dough Press. Extrude strands for the hair, brush edible glue all over the head and attach the hair in layers until you have the desired style.

Girl in the Spotted Dress

1. Use circle cutters 2 and 3 from the Spacer and Sizing Cutter set. Cut out two no. 3 size circles, one for the head and one for the legs, from Flesh Sugar Dough. Cut out a no. 3 circle for the body and a no. 2 circle for the arms from White Sugar Dough. Place the circles underneath a floppy mat to keep them from drying out.

2. Roll a cone for the body and insert a piece of raw spaghetti down through the centre, leaving 3cm showing at the top to support the head. Make the legs and add black shoes with straps. Position the legs on the body so that the girl is sitting cross-legged. Use foam to support the knees until they are dry.

3. Cut out a no. 4 circle of White Sugar Dough for the skirt and cut out a 1.5cm circle from the centre. Place this over the body and secure around the waistline with edible glue. Paint the spots on the dress with Poinsettia Liquid Food Colour then leave to dry.

4. Cut out a narrow strip of Red Sugar Dough for the sash and secure this around her waist. Use a cutting wheel or tool no. 4 to cut a strip for the bow measuring approximately 8cm x 1cm. Cut this piece in half and fold the two halves over. Cut the raw edges on both pieces into a point, stick them together and add a small ball in the middle. Make two bow tails, fix these to the sash then add the bow on top.

5. Make the arms from the prepared white circle, bend each arm at the elbow and secure to the top of the body. Push a piece of raw spaghetti through the wrist and support the arms with foam until they are set. Paint some dots on the sleeves and leave to dry. Make two hands from 5g of Flesh Sugar Dough. Make a straight cut at the wrist and apply some edible glue then slip over the spaghetti in the arm.

6. Roll the circle for the head into a smooth ball, then pull out the neck area and shape the chin. Make a straight cut at the base of the neck and indent the eye area with the side of your little finger. Add the nose, ears and a small, round hole

Girl in the Blue Dress

1. Use circle cutter no. 3 to cut out one circle from Flesh Sugar Dough for the head, one from Blue Sugar Dough for the body, and one from White Sugar Dough for the legs. Cut out one Blue Sugar Dough circle with the no. 2 cutter for the arms.

2. Make the body, legs and shoes as before. Cut out one no. 4 circle from White Sugar Dough for the petticoat then frill the edges with a cocktail stick. Cut out the centre with the small circle cutter and slip it over the body. Cut out another no. 4 circle from Blue Sugar Dough for the skirt, frill the edges as before then remove the centre and arrange it over the petticoat.

3. Paint a pattern with Bluebell Liquid Food Colour on the legs. The shoes and hands are made as previously described.

4. Colour 10g of White Sugar Dough with a little Marigold Paste Food Colour then extrude strands of this from the Sugar Dough Press for the hair. Twist two or three short strands together to make one curl. Brush the head with edible glue and cover it with curls.

5. Make a bow from 5g of Red Sugar Dough. Roll two small cone shapes, place them with the pointed ends together on top of the hair and add a small ball in the centre.

Boy in the Green Jacket

1. Mix 20g of Blue Sugar Dough with 80g of White Sugar Dough and roll it out. Cut out two no. 3 circles for the legs (you will need to two for the trousers) and one no. 3 circle for the body. Cut out two no. 2 circles from 10g of Green Sugar Dough for the arms and one no. 3 circle of Flesh Sugar Dough for the head.

2. Assemble the body and legs as before but add stitch marks along the sides of the trouser legs and up the front of the body to the waist.

3. Roll out 20g of Green Sugar Dough for the jacket. Cut a rectangle measuring 7cm x 4cm then apply a little edible glue around the body and wrap the paste around it, leaving an opening at the front. Turn the top edge over for the collar and attach two small squares for the pockets. Make stitch marks on three sides of the pockets. Make the arms in the same way as before and secure them in place with edible glue. Support the bent arm with foam until dry. Add a small, White Sugar Dough collar at the neck.

4. Make and attach the hands and the head, this time adding a small tongue at the mouth.

5. Mix 10g of White Sugar Dough with a little Golden Bear Brown, soften with white vegetable fat and fill the Sugar Dough Press. Extrude the short strands for the hair and stick them to the head.

6. Make two shoes from 10g of Yellow Sugar Dough. Roll two oval shapes and use tool no. 4 to indent the join at the sole of the shoe. Roll a fine strip of Orange Sugar Dough to go around the shoe then fix the shoes to the bottom of the trouser legs. Add two thin shoelaces, one tied in a bow and the other undone with one end in the child's hand.

7. Attach a couple of patches to the trousers and jacket to complete the boy.

Boy with Glasses

1. Colour 100g of White Sugar Dough with Gentian Paste Food Colour. Roll out and cut three no. 3 circles (for the body and legs) and one no. 2 circle (for the arms). Roll out some Flesh Sugar Dough and cut out one no. 3 circle for the head.

2. Assemble the body and legs as before. Make the shoes from 10g of Brown Sugar Dough, trimmed with a thin

strip of Golden Bear Brown Sugar Dough. Secure all these pieces together with edible glue.

3. Cut out two 4cm squares from 25g of Golden Bear Brown Sugar Dough for the back and front of the jumper. Make a diagonal cut at the seams of the sleeves then either mark on stitching or paint on a pattern with Liquid Food Colour. Arrange the two squares so that the seams meet at either side of the body and secure with edible glue.

4. Roll the no. 2 circle into a sausage shape for the arms and shape as before. Attach them in place with edible glue and add two small, square patches for decoration. Make the hands as previously described.

5. Roll a ball for the head and proceed to shape as before. Indent a smile with tool no. 11 and then straighten the top lip out by inserting tool no. 2. Make two tiny white teeth and stick them in place.

Finishing Touches

TIP When you have a piece to put into place that is too small to pick up with your fingers, put some edible glue on the end of a paintbrush and use it to pick up the piece and place it in the required position.

1. Stick all the figures to the cake with edible glue.

2. Model a small teddy bear from 15g of Golden Bear Brown Sugar Dough (see page 12 to 13 for instructions). Once complete, stick the teddy bear beside the girl in the spotted dress.

6. Twist a length of gold floristry wire around a pencil to make one lens of the glasses. Make a few twists for the bridge then twist the wire around the pencil again to make the second lens. Trim off any excess wire and position the glasses over the nose.

7. Make the hair from 10g of Golden Bear Brown Sugar Dough in the same way as for the other boy.

8. Dust the cheeks with Pastel Pink Dust Food Colour and add a few freckles using a no. 0 paintbrush dipped in Marigold Liquid Food Colour.

Skating in the Park

Children love playing in the snow, so this winter-themed cake would be perfect for a seasonal birthday party or would make a great talking point for your Christmas table.

Materials

20.5cm (8") round cake

1.1kg (2lb 7oz) white sugarpaste

SK Sugar Dough: 135g (4³/₄oz) Black, 25g (1oz) Brown, 35g (1¹/₄oz) Flesh, 10g (¹/₃oz) Golden Bear Brown, 150g (5¹/₄oz) Red and 50g (1³/₄oz) White

SK Paste Food Colour: Cactus

SK Pastel Dust Colour: Pastel Pink

SK Liquid Food Colours: Bulrush and Sunflower

135g (4³/₄oz) SK Instant Mix Pastillage

100g (3¹/₂oz) SK Instant Mix Royal Icing

SK Confectioners' Glaze

SK Edible Glue

Raw spaghetti

White vegetable fat

Icing sugar (in shaker)

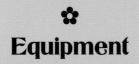

Equipment

30.5cm (12") round cake drum

Non-stick board and rolling pin

SK Modelling Tools

SK Spacers and Sizing Cutters

SK Sugar Dough Press

SK Paintbrushes: nos. 0 and 10

Circle cutters: small (CT)

Palette knife: small

Cocktail stick

Template (see page 107)

Covering the Cake and Board

1. Roll out 500g of white sugarpaste and cover the board. Allow to firm.

2. Cover the cake using the remaining white sugarpaste. Allow to firm, then secure the cake towards the back of the board.

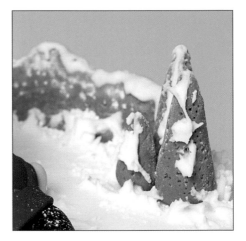

3. Make the frieze using 50g of White Sugar Dough coloured with Cactus Paste Food Colour. Use the template as a guide to cut out the shape, then prick the surface with a cocktail stick. Dust the surface with icing sugar and remove the excess with your finger, leaving some inside the holes. Glue the frieze to the back of the cake in a semi-circle.

4. Make up some royal icing to a soft peak consistency. Using a small palette knife, apply rough icing around the back and front of the frieze to support it. Make some cone-shaped trees in different sizes and prick these all over with cocktail sticks. Secure the trees beside the frieze with little icing and add some icing down the sides of the trees and along the top of the frieze. Finally, dust with icing sugar to resemble snow.

Skates

1. Make up 70g of pastillage and model three pairs of white boots using approximately half the paste. Mark around the edge of each boot with tool no. 4 to make the sole and heel. Push a short piece of raw spaghetti into the top of each boot.

2. To make the blades, roll out the remaining pastillage quite thinly and cut a rectangle for each boot measuring 2.5cm x 1cm. Cut a curve from the top using a 3cm round cutter and round off the corners. Leave the blades and boots to dry for 12 hours and then attach a blade to each boot using a strong glue made from pastillage powder mixed to a

stiff paste with edible glue. Set the completed boots aside until dry.

Sledge

1. Roll out 15g of pastillage and cut out a rectangle for the top of the sledge measuring 7cm x 3.5cm. Roll out a further 50g of pastillage between two spacers and cut out two strips for the runners measuring 7cm x 1.5cm. Make diagonal cuts at each end and cut out two square shapes along the top edge. Place all the pieces flat and leave to dry overnight, turning once.

2. Paint the top of the sledge with a mixture of Bulrush and Sunflower Liquid Food Colours and set aside to dry. Secure the runners to the top using strong sugar glue.

Sitting Girl

1. Roll 15g of Red Sugar Dough into a cone shape for the body and push a piece of raw spaghetti down through the centre, leaving 3cm showing at the top. Position the body so that it is leaning backwards. Roll 15g of Black Sugar Dough into a sausage shape for the legs, make a diagonal cut in the centre and bend slightly

at the knees. Secure the legs to the body and attach the skates to the legs using edible glue.

2. Make the jacket using 20g of Red Sugar Dough, divide in half and roll out a piece measuring 4.5cm x 5cm. Narrow the jacket at the shoulders and secure to the back of the body with the seams down the sides of the body. Cut a second piece for the front of the jacket measuring 7cm x 4cm and narrow the sides to the neck. Place this on the front of the body, joining the side seams neatly. Cut a strip to go around the bottom edge of the jacket. Using a 5mm round cutter, cut out the buttons and attach them to the front of the jacket.

3. Make two hands from Flesh Sugar Dough. Using tool no. 4, cut a 'V' shape for the thumb and cut the four fingers. Round off the edges and set aside. Make the arms from 10g of Red Sugar Dough, attach the hands to the ends and secure to the shoulders using edible glue. Position the arms behind the figure with the palms facing downwards. Trim the end of the sleeves with a strip of Red Sugar Dough.

4. Roll 15g of Flesh Sugar Dough into a ball for the head and pull out the neck underneath. Lay the head in the palm

of your hand and indent the eye area with the side of your little finger. Gently push up the chin area to make a crescent-shaped ridge underneath the eyes. Add a small oval shape for the nose and push the end of a paintbrush into the mouth area.

5. Indent the eyelids using tool no. 11 and outline the eyes and eyebrows using a no. 0 paintbrush and Bulrush Liquid Food Colour. Dust the cheeks with Pastel Pink Dust Food Colour and a soft brush. Make two small teardrop shapes for the ears and secure to the side of the head by pressing the end of a paintbrush into the bottom of the ear.

6. Apply some edible glue around the head and soften 10g of Golden Bear Brown Sugar Dough with white vegetable fat. Extrude the paste through a Sugar Dough Press and take off a few strands at the time using a cocktail stick. Apply the hair to the head, starting at the back and working around to the front. Make a straight cut at the neck, apply some edible glue and slip the head over the spaghetti at the neck. Cut a small strip of Red Sugar Dough for the collar and trim the cuffs on the sleeves. Add a red hat.

Second Girl

1. Roll 15g of Black Sugar Dough into a cone shape for the body and lay this down on the work surface. Make the legs from a further 15g of Black Sugar Dough. Bend both legs at the knees and secure to the body. Secure the skates into the bottom of the legs with edible glue. Support with foam if necessary until they are dry.

2. To make the back of the jacket, roll out 10g of Red Sugar Dough and cut out a 5cm square. Taper each side to fit around the body. Secure as before and tuck it in at the sides. (There is no need to make the front.)

3. Make the arms from 10g of Red Sugar Dough and place them in front of the body. Add two hands using Flesh Sugar Dough and position them with the palms facing downwards.

4. Model the head from 15g of Flesh Sugar Dough as previously described but this time add small, white balls for the eyes and black pupils. Using a no. 0 paintbrush and some Bulrush Liquid Food Colour, outline the eyes, eyelashes and eyebrows. Make the hair as before using 10g of Brown Sugar Dough. Top with a small, round hat made from Red Sugar Dough and mould it to fit the top of the head.

Dog

1. You will require 25g of Black Sugar Dough to complete the dog. Begin by rolling 10g into a cone for the body. Make two small cones for the back legs and secure these to the back of the body. Add two small balls for the back feet.

2. To make the head, make a cone from 10g of paste and flatten the front slightly. Mark down the centre using tool no. 4. Push a paintbrush into the mouth to make a hole and add a small, pink tongue. Add a round, black nose and glue it to the top of the snout. Make two holes for the eyes with the end of a paintbrush and add two small, white balls of paste. Make two small banana shapes for the eyebrows and glue these above the eyes. Paint on the pupils using a no. 0 paintbrush and Bulrush Liquid Food Colour.

3. Roll a tail from a tapered sausage shape, make a diagonal cut at one end secure to the back of the dog. Make

two flattened cone shapes for the ears and glue in place. Sit the dog at the back of the figure.

4. Make two front legs from Black Sugar Dough and shape the paw so that it looks thicker than the leg. Make a straight cut at the top of the leg and push a piece of raw spaghetti into it. Glue the legs to the dog so that the paw rests on top of the girl and mark the paws using tool no. 4.

Boy on the Sledge

1. Using Brown, Red and Black Sugar Dough, make and assemble the boy on the sledge as previously described using the same proportions of paste as for the girl lying down. To make the hair, extrude short strands of softened Black Sugar Dough from the Sugar Dough Press and glue them around the head.

2. Make the head as for the lying down girl, but add some teeth and lips. To make the teeth, mark the smile using tool no. 11 then take the curve out of the top, making it straight. Add a small banana shape in White Sugar Dough and glue this to the top of the mouth. Add two small cone shapes for the upper lip and a small banana shape for the lower lip.

Dog on the Sledge

Make the dog as previously described using 20g of Black Sugar Dough. For this dog, you will not require any back legs. Add a small strip of red for his collar.

Finishing Touches

1. Highlight the eyes and noses on the dogs with confectioners' glaze.

2. Add some royal icing here and there and dust with icing sugar.

Materials

20.5cm (8") square cake

800g (1lb 12oz) white sugarpaste

SK Sugar Dough: 15g ($^1/_2$oz) Black, 30g (1oz) Blue, 40g (1$^1/_2$oz) Brown, 475g (1lb 1oz) Golden Bear Brown and 400g (14oz) White

SK Paste Food Colours: Poinsettia and Sunflower

SK Liquid Food Colours: Bluebell and Bulrush

SK Scintilloes Piping Sparkles: Blue

SK Gum Tragacanth

SK Confectioners' Glaze

SK Edible Glue

Raw spaghetti

❁

Equipment

25.5cm (10") square cake drum

Non-stick board and rolling pin

SK Modelling Tools

SK Spacers and Sizing Cutters

SK Paintbrush: no. 0

Circle cutters: small (CT)

Heart cutters (KT)

Basket weave pattern rolling pin (PME)

Templates (see page 106 and 107)

Puppy Love

There is a new puppy in the house and he is causing all tails to wag! You could recreate this cake with a model of your own dog on the top or perhaps the dog of the recipient.

Covering the Cake and Board

1. Colour 800g of sugarpaste with Sunflower Paste Food Colour to make a pale lemon shade. Use 350g to cover the board and use the rest to cover the cake. Secure the cake to the centre of the board.

2. Make the bones for the border at the base of the cake. Take 100g of White Sugar Dough and split it into several small balls of equal size. Shape the balls into ovals then roll them backwards and forwards on the work surface to narrow them in the centre. Mark the bone at each end with tool no. 4. Position the bones around three sides of the cake, securing with edible glue. Set aside three bones for the front of the cake.

'Woof' Lettering

1. Mix 20g of Blue Sugar Dough with 220g of White Sugar Dough to make a pale blue shade. Reserve about 40g of this paste for later use. Strengthen the remaining pale blue Sugar Dough by kneading in $^1/_2$tsp of gum tragacanth.

2. Use the spacers to roll out the pale blue Sugar Dough evenly. Use the template provided to cut out the word 'woof' then leave the letters to dry on a flat surface, turning them over once.

3. Paint paw prints on the letters using Bluebell Liquid Food Colour and a no. 0 paintbrush then leave to dry. Secure the letters to the front of the cake and add the little bones in-between the letters.

Dog Basket

1. Use the spacers to roll out 100g of Golden Bear Brown Sugar Dough. Cut out an oval shape using the template.

2. Roll out a further 100g of Golden Bear Brown Sugar Dough between the spacers and cut a strip measuring 23cm x 3cm. Round off each end of the strip. Roll over the top of the strip once with the basket weave rolling pin then cut the long edges straight. Stick the strip around the edge of the oval base and set aside to dry.

Puppy

1. Roll 30g of Golden Bear Brown Sugar Dough into a ball for the body. Shape the ball into a cone shape and push a piece of raw spaghetti down through the centre, leaving 2cm showing at the top.

2. Roll out 20g of the reserved pale blue Sugar Dough and cut out two rectangles measuring about 2cm x 1cm for the t-shirt. Attach one rectangle to the front and one to the back of the body, then use tool no. 4 to mark the side seams.

3. Roll out 15g of White Sugar Dough and cut out a rectangle measuring 12cm x 6cm. Cut out the shape for the nappy using the template. Sit the body in the centre of this piece and bring the centre point up at the front of the body and the ends around the side to cross over at the front. Secure in position with a little edible glue.

4. Roll 15g of Golden Bear Brown Sugar Dough into a sausage shape and turn up the ends to make the shape for the back legs. Cut in half with a straight cut then mark the paws with tool no. 4. Add two brown pads for the paws and fix the legs to the base of the body.

5. Make the sleeves from a small sausage of the pale blue Sugar Dough. Make a diagonal cut in the centre and a straight cut at each end. Roll 10g of Golden Bear Brown Sugar Dough into a sausage shape for the arms. Make a straight cut in the centre and stick this straight edge to the bottom of the sleeves. Fix the sleeves to the top of the body and use tool no. 4 to mark the paws.

6. Roll 20g of Golden Bear Brown Sugar Dough into a ball for the head and mould a slight cone shape at the front. Slip this over the spaghetti at the neck and secure with edible glue. Add a small ball of Brown Sugar Dough for the snout and mark the centre with tool no. 4. Make a hole at the top of the snout and insert a small Black Sugar Dough cone for the nose. Make a hole for the mouth with the end of a paintbrush

7. Roll two small balls of White Sugar Dough for the eyes and stick them in place with edible glue. Add two small Black Sugar Dough balls for the pupils and flatten with your finger. Add two small eyebrows and draw an outline around the eyes with Bulrush Liquid Food Colour.

8. Roll two small Brown Sugar Dough cones for the ears and place them flat against the head. Use more Brown Sugar Dough to make small circles for the spots on the puppy.

9. Mix 20g of White Sugar Dough with a little Poinsettia Paste Food Colour to make the pink for the hat. Roll it out and cut a 4cm circle then roll this out a little wider and make a straight cut at the base. Stick it to the puppy's head. Make two small ties and two loops for the bow then attach these to the front with edible glue. Position the basket and the finished puppy on top of the cake.

Sitting Dog

1. Roll 40g of Golden Bear Brown Sugar Dough into a cone shape for the body and push a piece of raw spaghetti down through the centre, leaving 2cm at the top to support the head.

2. Roll a sausage shape from 15g of Golden Bear Brown Sugar Dough then make a diagonal cut in the centre. Bend the two pieces into the shape for the hind legs and make a straight cut at the end. Secure the legs to the side of the body using edible glue. Add two small balls of White Sugar Dough for the paws and mark the paws with tool no. 4.

3. Roll 10g of Golden Bear Brown Sugar Dough into a sausage shape, make a straight cut at each end and a diagonal cut in the centre to make the front legs. Cut off a small piece at a steep angle to make the top of the legs thinner. Stick the legs to the front of the body then add two paws as before.

4. Roll a small amount of White Sugar Dough into a cone shape then flatten it with your fingers. Use tool no. 4 to mark downward strokes to resemble fur. Attach this to the front of the body, covering the top of the legs.

5. Roll 20g of Golden Bear Brown Sugar Dough into a ball for the head and indent around the eye area with your finger. Place the head over the spaghetti at the neck and secure with edible glue. Roll two small cone shapes made from 5g of White Sugar Dough and place them in

position on the face for the cheeks. Mark the fur with tool no. 4 then make a small banana shape from Golden Bear Brown Sugar Dough and fix this underneath the cheeks. Roll a small tongue from pink coloured Sugar Dough and stick this inside the mouth, then mark down the centre with tool no. 4.

6. Divide 5g of Brown Sugar Dough in half to make the ears. Roll each piece into a cone shape and make a straight cut at the narrow end. Push a piece of raw spaghetti into each side of the head and slip the narrow end of the ears over this, securing to the head with edible glue. Add a tuft of hair and mark with tool no. 4.

7. Roll out some Brown Sugar Dough, cut out a 1.5cm circle then attach it to the head for the patch around the left eye. Cut out two 1cm circles from White Sugar Dough and place one over the brown circle and the other one directly on the head for the right eye. Add two small, black

circles on top for the pupils. Paint on the eyebrows with Bulrush Liquid Food Colour then add a couple of spots on the body.

8. Roll a small cone from Brown Sugar Dough for the tail, make a diagonal cut at the thickest end and secure to the back of the body. Mark the hair on the tail with tool no. 4. Position the dog at the back of the cake.

Crouching Dog

Make this dog as described for the sitting dog and shape the body, legs and tail into the correct positions. The tail for this dog has been pulled out from the Sugar Dough body.

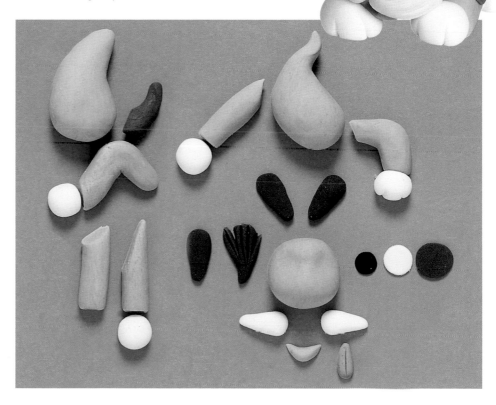

Dog at the Front

1. Make four paws as before, three from Golden Bear Brown Sugar Dough and one from White. Stick them to the two 'O's with edible glue. Add two Brown Sugar Dough pads to the back paws.

2. Make a flat cone shape from White Sugar Dough for the chest fur and mark with tool no. 4 as before. Stick this in-between the two 'O's.

3. Make the head as before then push a piece of raw spaghetti into the cake. Add a little edible glue and push the head over the spaghetti.

Finishing Touches

1. To make the bottle, roll 5g of White Sugar Dough into a sausage shape and make a straight cut at each end. Add a small Brown Sugar Dough cone shape on top for the teat, secure with edible glue, then position this inside the basket. Make a small, white ball and a smaller pink ball then place one on top of the other for the dummy. Stick this over the mouth of the puppy.

2. Make a small, pink dog collar and wrap it around the letter 'W',

securing it in place with edible glue. Make a small, grey buckle, stick this to the front of the collar then decorate the collar with two pink hearts and two smaller red hearts.

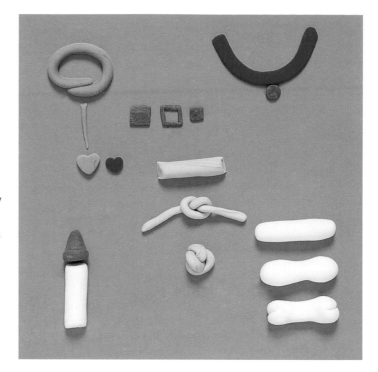

3. Make a ball by rolling together small pieces of Sugar Dough in several colours. To make the chewing bone, mix 5g of White Sugar Dough with a little Golden Bear Brown Sugar Dough, roll it into a sausage shape and cut a short length for the centre. Roll two thin strips from the remaining pieces, knot them together then fix them to both ends of the central piece.

4. Make a red collar for the sitting dog from White Sugar Dough mixed with Poinsettia Paste Food Colour. Cut out a thin strip and fix loosely around the neck, then attach a small, grey disc to the front.

5. To make the dog bowl, roll 15g of pale blue Sugar Dough into a ball and flatten it with your fingers. Make a well in the centre and fill it with Blue Scintilloes Piping Sparkles. Add a trim of pink around the top and paint on some paw prints with Bluebell Liquid Food Colour.

6. Brush the puppies' eyes and noses with confectioners' glaze to add a shine.

A Day at Camp

Some boys like nothing better than to get wet and dirty, to fish and play with grubs – all in a day's work at this camp!

Covering the Cake and Board

1. Colour 1.1kg of sugarpaste with Mint Paste Food Colour. Use this paste to cover the board, followed by the cake. Secure the cake off-centre on the board, leaving more space at the front.

2. Soften 60g of Green Sugar Dough with white vegetable fat and fill the cup of a Sugar Dough Press. Extrude short strands in clumps and arrange around the base of the cake for grass.

Pond and Rocks

1. Make the pond using 100g of White Sugar Dough marbled with 20g of Blue Sugar Dough (see page 11). Roll out the paste and make an irregular shape to fit the front of the board. In the centre of the pond, make a round ripple shape using a flattened ball of Sugar Dough, and smooth into a circular shape with tool no. 1.

2. To make the rocks, you will need 40g of White Sugar Dough and 10g of Black. Make a solid grey colour but leave some black and white. Marble the three colours together randomly and pull off pieces of paste, leaving a rough edge. Arrange them around the edge of the pond. Add a few strands of grass as previously described.

3. Add a little clear alcohol to thin the Blue Scintilloes down. Apply a thin coat of the diluted Scintilloes to the surface of the pond and stones to add a shine.

Fish

1. Model a fish as shown from 5g of Flesh Sugar Dough. Mark the fish with scales using tool no. 11 and add small, black dots for the eyes. Make a small but deep hole for the mouth for the end of the line to be inserted into later.

Materials

15cm x 20.5cm (6" x 8") oval cake

1.2kg (2lb 10oz) white sugarpaste

SK Sugar Dough: 20g ($^3/_4$oz) Black, 65g (2$^1/_4$oz) Blue, 20g ($^3/_4$oz) Brown, 110g (4oz) Flesh, 80g (2$^3/_4$oz) Golden Bear Brown, 75g (2$^1/_2$oz) Green, 20g ($^3/_4$oz) Orange, 60g (2oz) Red, 320g (11$^1/_4$oz) White and 30g (1oz) Yellow

SK Paste Food Colour: Mint

SK Designer Dust Colour: Lichen Glow

SK Metallic Lustre Dust: Silver

SK Pastel Dust Colour: Pastel Pink

SK Liquid Food Colours: Bulrush and Poinsettia

100g (3$^1/_2$oz) SK Instant Mix Pastillage

SK Scintilloes Piping Sparkles: Blue

SK Edible Glue

Unbreakable gel: clear (OP)

Raw spaghetti

White vegetable fat

Clear alcohol

❀

Equipment

30.5cm (12") petal-shaped drum

Non-stick board and rolling pin

SK Modelling Tools

SK Spacers and Sizing Cutters

SK Sugar Dough Press

SK Paintbrush: no. 00

24 gauge floristry wire

Piping bag

Piping nozzle: no. 3

Templates (see page 106)

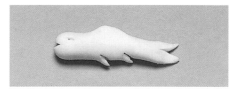

2. Dust the fish with Silver Metallic Lustre Dust. Cut the fish in half and place the top half in the centre of the ripple and the other at the back of the sitting boy.

Frog

Roll 10g of Green Sugar Dough into a cone shape for the body and make a rounded part at the top for the head. Place this on the rock. Roll the back and front legs, making the back legs slightly thicker, and make the webbed feet with tool no. 4. Using a soft brush, mark the skin with patches of Bulrush Liquid Food Colour. When dry, apply and thin coat of Blue Scintilloes to make the frog look wet.

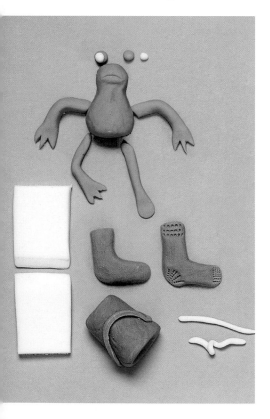

Dog

Roll 15g of Golden Bear Brown Sugar Dough roll into a cone shape. Roll the pointed end between your fingers to shape the tail. Make two small cone shapes for the back legs and round off the feet, marking the paws with tool no. 4. Add a few spots using Brown Sugar Dough.

Tent

1. Roll out 80g of pastillage and cut two 8cm squares. Cut along the top edge of both pieces so that the edge slants inwards – when dry, the pieces will fit together to create a mitred corner with a point at the top. Lay the pieces on a flat surface to dry and leave for 12 hours before turning over to dry on the other side. When dry, fix the pieces together along the mitred edge using strong edible glue.

2. For the tent covering, mix 90g of White Sugar Dough with 35g of Blue Sugar Dough to make a denim colour. Using the template, cut out two triangles for the front and back of the tent. Divide the front in half and secure with edible glue, leaving an opening for the figures. Secure the back piece in position.

3. Roll out the remaining blue paste and cut out a rectangle measuring of 11cm x 17cm for the top of the tent. Try it first to see if it fits correctly – it should overlap slightly at the front and back – then attach with edible glue. Place the finished tent on top of the cake. Lift up the edge of the tent and place the dog underneath.

4. Model two grey socks and mark stitching on the top, heel and toe using tool no. 12. Brush one side with a little edible glue and drape them over the tent.

Boy in the Tent

1. Roll 20g of Orange Sugar Dough into a cone shape for the body. Roll 15g of Brown Sugar Dough into a sausage shape and make a straight cut in the centre and at both ends. Bend one leg slightly and attach to the body. Push a small piece of raw spaghetti into the end of each leg.

2. Roll two ovals of Yellow Sugar Dough for the shoes and add a flattened oval of Golden Bear Brown Sugar Dough for each sole. Mark the heel and sole with tool no. 4. Apply a little glue to the underside of the body and slip it inside the tent, then attach the shoes to the legs with edible glue. Support the bent leg with a little foam until dry.

Bucket of Worms

1. Mix 10g of White Sugar Dough with 5g of Black to make a grey shade. Reserve a little paste for the handle, then roll the remaining paste into a short sausage shape to make the bucket. Hollow out the centre using tool no. 3 and paint on the word 'Worms' using a no. 00 paintbrush and some Bulrush Liquid Food Colour. Make a thin strip for the handle and secure to either side of the bucket.

2. Roll out tiny strips of Flesh Sugar Dough and curl them up to make the worms. Glue some inside and outside the bucket and a few by the pond.

Fishing Rod

1. To make the handle, roll 5g of Golden Bear Brown Sugar Dough into a sausage and cut to measure 4cm. Push a length of 24 gauge wire down through the centre and curve it. Make some loops by rolling small balls of White Sugar Dough and pushing the end of a paintbrush through the centre. Glue them along the wire.

2. Make up some unbreakable gel for the line following the instructions on the packet and allow to stand for four hours. Place the gel into a piping bag with a no. 3 nozzle and pipe a line onto a non-stick board or sheet of acetate, making it long enough to reach from the handle to the fish. When dry, carefully remove from the board or acetate and thread through the loops on the fishing rod. Push the line into the end of the handle and add a small circle of White Sugar Dough to secure.

Boy with Fishing Rod

1. Make two ovals for the shoes from 15g of Golden Bear Brown Sugar Dough and add stitch marks around the bottom to form a sole. Take the stitch marks up from this line to the front of the shoes, as shown.

2. Roll 20g of Flesh Sugar Dough into a sausage shape for the legs, make a diagonal cut in the centre and a straight cut at each end. Push a piece of raw spaghetti down through the centre of each leg, apply a little glue to the top of the shoes and glue the legs on top. Leave some spaghetti showing at the top of each leg.

3. Roll 25g of Red Sugar Dough into a cone shape for the body. Apply some glue to the top of the legs and slip the body over the spaghetti. Set aside to dry before dressing. Cut a small strip of White Sugar Dough for the socks and wrap around the ankle. Join neatly at the back, securing with edible glue. Paint them in a check design using a no. 00 paintbrush and some Poinsettia Liquid Food Colour.

4. Mix 15g of White Sugar Dough with 10g of Blue Sugar Dough to make a denim colour. Roll out the paste and make the dungarees using the templates as a

guide. Secure the front and back to the body, making sure they meet neatly at the side seams. Add stitch marks on either side and add a patch pocket on the back.

5. To make the sleeves, roll 15g of Red Sugar Dough into a sausage shape, make a diagonal cut in the centre and trim to size. Push a short piece of raw spaghetti into the straight end. Model the lower arms and hands from 10g of Flesh Sugar Dough and secure them to the sleeves. Add a red cuff to cover the join. Attach the arms to the top of the body and bring them forward into a natural position, then secure with edible glue.

6. Cut two straps for the dungarees, cross them over at the back and finish with two small buckles. Add small red buttons to the front and a small strap and button on the side of each leg. Make a collar from Red Sugar Dough and secure in place with edible glue.

7. Roll 20g of Flesh Sugar Dough into a ball for the head, pull the neck out at the base and make the mouth by inserting the end of a paintbrush. Roll a small cone for the nose and smooth it into place, then make two small holes for the nostrils. Roll a small banana shape for the bottom lip and secure in place. Add two small teardrop shapes for the ears and indent with the end of a paintbrush. Roll two small, white balls for the eyes and add brown pupils. Outline the eyes using a no. 00 paintbrush with Bulrush Liquid Food Colour.

8. To make the hair, soften some Golden Bear Brown Sugar Dough and extrude the paste through a Sugar Dough Press. Brush the head with edible glue and arrange the hair in the desired style. To make the cap, roll out a little Red Sugar Dough and cut out a 3cm circle. Cut another circle for the peak and cut straight on each side. Place the cap onto the head and attach the peak.

9. Apply some glue to the palms of the boy's hands and attach the handle of the fishing rod firmly. Push the end of the fishing line into the mouth of the fish and secure with a little Sugar Dough and glue to prevent it from coming out.

Sitting Boy

1. Roll 30g of Golden Bear Brown Sugar Dough into an oval shape and make a slit in the centre for the legs. Roll the edges until they are rounded and sit the shape on top of the rock.

2. Push a short piece of raw spaghetti into the end of the trouser legs. Roll 20g of Flesh Sugar Dough into a sausage shape, make a straight cut at each end and bending at the knee. Brush the ends with edible glue and attach to the trousers so that the lower leg appears as if it has gone into the water. Add a small pocket at the back and mark with stitches.

3. Roll a cone from 20g of Yellow Sugar Dough for the upper body. Using your fingers, hollow out the lower edge and widen it into a bell shape, thinning the edge to make it wider than the trouser top. Place this over the trousers and then push a piece of raw spaghetti down through the centre and into the rock,

leaving 3cm showing at the top. Add stitch marks around the edge of the sweater. Make the arms and hands as before and position them resting on the legs.

4. Make the head in the same way as before. Give this boy brown hair and add some thicker curls at the front.

Finishing Touches

Using a dry, flat brush, dust the cheeks of the two boys with Pastel Pink Dust Food Colour. Dust the top of the cake and board lightly with Lichen Glow Designer Dust Colour. Finally, make a small ball by rolling together oddments of the colours you are using. Secure the ball next to the dog.

Materials

15cm x 20.5cm (6" x 8") oval cake

1.46kg (3lb 3oz) white sugarpaste

SK Sugar Dough: 75g (2³/₄oz) Flesh and 70g (2¹/₂oz) White

SK Paste Food Colours: Blackberry, Bluebell, Edelweiss and Teddy Bear Brown

SK Metallic Lustre Dust: Silver

SK Pastel Dust Colour: Pastel Pink

SK Magic Sparkle Dust

SK Liquid Food Colours: Bulrush and Marigold

SK Edible Glue

Raw spaghetti

Clear alcohol

❀

Equipment

25.5cm x 30.5cm (10" x 12") oval cake drum

Non-stick board and rolling pin

SK Modelling Tools

SK Spacers and Sizing Cutters

SK Paintbrushes: nos. 0 and 10

Garrett frill cutter (FMM)

CelStick (CC) or cocktail stick

23cm (9") dot rolling pin (CC)

Flower former

This delightful christening or 'new baby' cake can be adapted to celebrate the arrival of a baby girl or boy. The baby and teddy bear can also be taken off the cake as a keepsake from the celebrations.

Shaping the Cake

Stand the cake on a piece of greaseproof paper. Using a sharp knife, carefully hollow out the top of the cake.

Covering the Cake and Board

1. Roll out 300g of white sugarpaste and cover the board in the usual way.

2. Roll out 600g of white sugarpaste into an oval shape and cover the cake. Carefully push the paste into the hollow in the top of the cake. Place the cake centrally on the board and dust around the board liberally with Magic Sparkle Dust. Leave to dry.

Cot

1. To make the lower frilled skirt for the cot, roll out 220g of sugarpaste and then cut it into long strips measuring 4cm wide. Working with one strip at a time, gently fold the paste to resemble material and attach it around the base of the cake with edible glue. Join each strip side by side so that it looks like one continuous piece of material.

2. For the next layer, roll out 320g of sugarpaste and cut into long strips measuring 9cm wide. Take one strip at a time and texture the surface with the dot rolling pin. Trim the lower edge straight, fold the strips as before and attach to the side of the cake. Make sure that the top of this layer goes right over the top of the cake.

3. Using a Garrett frill cutter set on narrow, make a frill to go around the top of the cake. Roll a CelStick or cocktail stick backwards and forwards over the edge of the paste to make a frill. Lift each alternate scallop and secure to the cake using edible glue. Repeat this process so that the frill goes around the cake, ensuring the joins are neat.

4. Roll a very fine shoelace strip of sugarpaste to go around the straight edge of the Garrett frill and attach in place with edible glue. Make a few loops and two shorter laces to decorate the side of the cot.

5. Make two letters using a small piece of the shoelace-thin sugarpaste: I have chosen 'W' for William but you can, of course, personalise the cake at this stage. Colour the letters with Silver Metallic Lustre Dust mixed with a little clear alcohol. Place one at the base of the cot and set one aside to attach to the pillow later.

Pillow

Form 20g of sugarpaste into a small, flat oblong shape. Roll out 25g of sugarpaste and cut out a rectangle slightly bigger than the oblong, then frill the edges using a CelStick or cocktail stick. Attach the frilled paste to the oblong and place the finished pillow at the top of the cot. Indent the pillow where the baby's head will rest with the end of a rolling pin.

William

1. Roll 40g of Flesh Sugar Dough into a cone shape to form the body. Mark a tummy button with tool no. 5.

2. Colour 70g of White Sugar Dough with a little Bluebell Paste Food Colour. Roll out 20g to make the top of the pyjama trousers. Cut out a 5cm circle and take out a small 'V' shape from the centre to the edge. Place the circle around the base of the body, leaving the gap at the front to show the tummy button. Tuck in the paste around the edges.

3. Roll 35g of the blue coloured Sugar Dough into a sausage shape then make a diagonal cut in the centre for the legs. Attach each leg to the body and arrange into the required position. Push a small piece of raw spaghetti into the bottom of each leg. Place the body inside the cot and secure in place with a little edible glue.

4. Cut out two 4cm squares of the blue coloured Sugar Dough for the pyjama top. Place each square on either side of the upper body and arrange them so that they come together at the top and open at the lower edge. Trim off any excess around the sides.

5. Divide 5g of Flesh Sugar Dough in half for the feet. Roll two oval shapes and flatten slightly, then use tool no. 4 to mark out the toes. Gently separate each toe and roll them between your fingers to round off the edges. Mark the toenails with the end of a piece of raw spaghetti. Attach the feet to the legs with edible glue.

6. Roll 25g of Flesh Sugar Dough into a smooth ball for the head and place into a flower former to ensure the head keeps its shape whilst you are modelling it. Indent a hole for the nose in the centre of the face using tool no. 5 and dab a touch of edible glue inside the hole. Roll a tiny cone shape for the nose and stick it into position. Mark a round mouth using tool no. 5, making the hole large enough to place the baby's thumb inside.

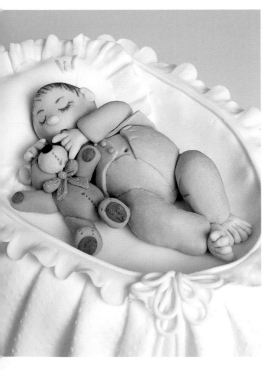

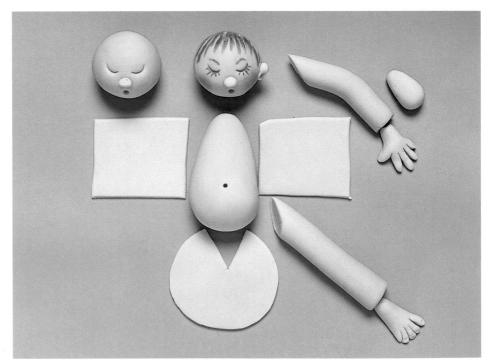

7. Mark the eyes with the small end of tool no. 11. Mix some Bulrush Liquid Food Colour with Marigold Liquid Food Colour (or use the colour of your choice) and paint on the facial features and hair with a no. 0 paintbrush. Brush the cheeks with Pastel Pink Dust. Place the completed head on top of the body, resting it on the pillow.

8. Roll a sausage from 15g of the blue Sugar Dough for the left arm only. Make a diagonal cut at one end and a straight cut at the other. Attach the arm to the top of the body, bringing it across the front, and push a piece of raw spaghetti into the wrist.

Teddy Bear

1. Colour 15g of White Sugar Dough with Teddy Bear Brown Paste Food Colour. Roll a small cone for the body then roll a small sausage shape for the legs. Turn the ends up for the feet and cut the sausage in half. Secure the legs to the body.

2. Roll a smaller sausage and cut it in half (with a diagonal cut) for the arms. Secure each arm to the top of the body. Make stitch marks on the body and feet using tool no. 13.

3. Roll a ball for the head, then add a snout and mark the centre with stitch marks. Roll a small cone of Blackberry coloured Sugar Dough for the nose and secure to the top of the snout. Use tool no. 5 to make a small round hole for the mouth. With the same tool, mark two eyes then

make stitch marks diagonally from each eye to where the ears will be. Roll two small balls for the ears, flatten them slightly and attach them to either side of the head. Fill the eyes with little balls of black coloured Sugar Dough. Add a little more Teddy Bear Brown Paste Food Colour to the paste for the bear to make a darker colour, then make tiny pads for the teddy's paws.

4. Add a small, blue bow under the teddy's chin and then paint on the spots using Edelweiss Paste Food Colour. Place the completed teddy bear by the side of the baby.

Hands

Divide 5g of Flesh Sugar Dough in half for the hands. Roll two cone shapes then cut out a 'V' where the thumb is. Mark out the remaining fingers and complete as instructed for the feet. Attach one hand over the spaghetti at the wrist, positioning the thumb inside the baby's mouth. Attach the other hand above the teddy's head.

Cool Cats

This design is ideal for a man or a woman's birthday, especially if the recipient enjoys a night out on the town like these cool cats.

Covering the Cake and Board

Cover the cake and board with white sugarpaste. Attach the cake to the board and set aside to dry.

Letters

1. Roll out 100g of Black Sugar Dough between the spacers (grooves facing upwards) and roll it out evenly. Use the templates to cut out the letters 'C', 'A' and 'S'. Smooth all around the raw edges then set the letters aside, keeping them flat until you are ready to decorate them.

2. To make the cat in the shape of the letter 'T', roll 30g of Black Sugar Dough into a flattened sausage shape for the body. It should measure about 6cm long. Position this on the side of the cake, securing with edible glue. Lightly mark the legs. Roll 15g of Black Sugar Dough into a sausage shape and make a diagonal cut in the centre for the arms. Secure the arms in position on the body; you may need to support them until they are dry.

3. Make two paws with fingers for the 'T' cat. Divide 10g of White Sugar Dough in two and roll these pieces into cone shapes. Flatten slightly then cut out a 'V' shape to create the thumb. Shape three fingers and roll them gently to soften the square edges. Stick each paw to the wrists with edible glue, ensuring the palms are facing upwards.

4. Roll four 15g pieces of Black Sugar Dough into balls for the heads. Place each head in the required position on the letters, securing with edible glue. Make small cone shapes for the ears and secure them in place. Make the cheeks from White Sugar Dough, position them on the face and use the end of a paintbrush to make a small hole for the mouth. Add two tiny White Sugar Dough cones for the eyes and two small banana shapes for the eyebrows.

5. Roll six 5g balls of White Sugar Dough for the front paws and eight slightly larger balls for the back paws. Apply a little edible glue and secure in the required position. Mark the paws using the rounded end of tool no. 4.

6. Make each tail from 5g of Black Sugar Dough rolled into a tapered sausage shape. Make a straight cut at the thick end then add a small tip of White Sugar Dough by rolling it over the thin end. Mark the tip with tool no. 4 and secure in place on the letter.

7. Add a small amount of Red Sugar Dough to 5g of White Sugar Dough to make a pink shade. Roll small cones for the inside of each ear, secure in place with edible glue and

Materials

25.5cm (10") round cake

1kg (2lb 3oz) white sugarpaste

SK Sugar Dough: 850g (1lb 14oz) Black, 10g ($^1/_2$oz) Red, 200g (7oz) White

SK Paste Food Colours: Bluebell and Edelweiss

SK Liquid Food Colour: Blackberry

65g (2oz) SK Instant Mix Pastillage

SK Edible Glue

Raw spaghetti

❀

Equipment

35.5cm (14") round cake drum

Non-stick board and rolling pin

SK Modelling Tools

SK Spacers and Sizing Cutters

SK Paintbrush: no. 0

Circle cutters: small (CT)

Floristry stamens: white

Templates (see page 107)

then smooth it out with tool no. 1. Apply a little edible glue to the mouths and insert pink tongues. Roll small pink cone shapes for the noses and indent two little nostrils using tool no. 5.

8. Mix a little Bluebell Paste Food Colour into 5g of White Sugar Dough to make a pale blue shade. Add a small ball of blue in each eye then put a tiny ball of Black Sugar Dough on top for the pupils. Highlight each eye by dipping a cocktail stick into Edelweiss Paste Food Colour and then dabbing it on the pupils. Add a few thin cone shapes of White Sugar Dough for the fur on top of the heads.

9. Cut three floristry stamens in half and remove the ends. Insert three pieces on either side of the cheeks to make the whiskers.

10. Once the completed letters are dry, position them on the side of the cake, spelling the word 'Cats'.

Paw Prints

Thinly roll out 25g of Black Sugar Dough and cut out several circles using the 1.5cm circle cutter. Make the smaller circles for the toe prints by hand-rolling four tiny balls of Black Sugar Dough and flattening them. Secure the paw prints in place on the board with edible glue.

Lamppost

1. Roll 20g of pastillage into a sausage shape 10cm long. Make a straight cut at either end. Push a piece of raw spaghetti through the centre, leaving some showing at each end, then leave to dry.

2. Use the spacers to roll out 50g of pastillage evenly, then cut out a 4cm and 3cm circle for the base of the lamppost. Set these aside to dry. Roll out the remaining pastillage thinner than before and cut out one 3cm circle for the top.

Make the globe by rolling 20g of White Sugar Dough into a ball. Place all the pieces on a flat surface to dry for 12 hours, turning them over halfway through.

3. Once all the pieces are dry, paint them with Blackberry Liquid Food Colour (excluding the globe) and leave to dry once again.

4. To assemble the lamppost, place the 4cm circle at the base with the 3cm circle on top. Push the spaghetti at the end of the post through the centre of both circles. Push the thin 3cm circle over the spaghetti at the top of the post, add the globe and secure in position with edible glue. Set aside to dry. Once dry, stick the lamppost into position on top of the cake using edible glue.

Cat with a Hat

1. Divide 15g of White Sugar Dough equally and roll it into two cone shapes for the feet. Mark the toes with tool no. 4.

2. Make the legs from 30g of Black Sugar Dough rolled into a sausage shape. Make a straight cut in the centre and at each end then push a piece of raw spaghetti down through each leg, leaving 3cm showing at the top and 1cm at the bottom. Apply a little edible glue to the bottom of the legs and push them into the feet. Cross the right leg over the left leg as shown and ensure that the tops of the legs are side-by-side and level.

3. Roll the body from 25g of Black Sugar Dough. Apply edible glue to the base and slip this over the spaghetti at the top of the legs. Ensure it is firmly in place then lean it over to the right a little and set it aside to dry.

4. Mould a small leaf shape from White Sugar Dough for the fur on the chest. Mark with tool no. 4 and stick it to the front of the body.

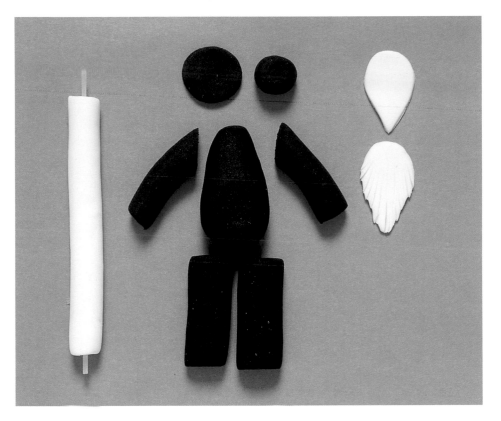

3. Roll 15g of Black Sugar Dough into a sausage shape and make the arms as before. Bend the right arm at the elbow so that the hand will be in an upright position. Secure to the top of the cat and rest it on the right leg. Make the hands as before, slip them over the spaghetti at the wrists and shape them as shown. The left arm is straight so push a piece of raw spaghetti through the centre and attach it to the body. Support this arm with foam until dry.

4. Make some white fur for the chest as before and stick it to the body. Complete the head, making sure that the eyes are looking to her left. Attach the head to the body with edible glue, so that she is looking upwards at the other cat.

5. Make two tails from 20g of Black Sugar Dough and add a white tip on the end of each. Secure one to the back of the female cat, curl it forward and rest it on her right leg. Stick the other tail to the back of the male cat and bring it forward to rest over the hand of the female cat, securing with edible glue.

5. Using 25g of Black Sugar Dough, model the head as previously described for the cats on the letters. Secure it over the spaghetti at the neck.

6. Make two hands as for the 'T' cat from 5g of White Sugar Dough and set aside. Make two arms from 15g of Black Sugar Dough and insert a length of raw spaghetti at each wrist. Bend the left arm at the elbow and secure to the top of the body, then secure the hand in place at the wrist and on the side of the body. Support with foam until dry. Attach the right arm and hand in place then apply SK Edible Glue to the hand and under the feet. Stand the cat next to the lamppost and wrap the right hand around the post to secure.

7. Make a small hat from 10g of Black Sugar Dough. Cut out a 1.5cm circle for the brim then roll the remainder into a small ball and fix it to the centre of the circle. Secure this to the cat's head in-between the ears and tilt it forwards.

8. Make a small bowtie from 5g of Red Sugar Dough. Secure the bow under the chin using edible glue.

Female Cat

1. Roll 25g of Black Sugar Dough into a slightly curved cone shape for the body. Position it at the base of the lamppost and push a piece of raw spaghetti down through the centre, leaving 3cm showing at the top.

2. Make the legs from 25g of Black Sugar Dough rolled into a sausage shape. Make them as before but roll them slimmer and longer than the other cat's legs. Stick the right leg to the body, bending it at the knee. Make two feet from 15g of White Sugar Dough divided equally and attach one to the end of the right leg with edible glue. Place the left leg over the right and push a piece of raw spaghetti into the end. Attach the foot, making it slightly pointed.

IMPORTANT NOTE Ensure the whiskers are removed from the cats before the cake is eaten.

Templates

The Farmer
Wants A Wife

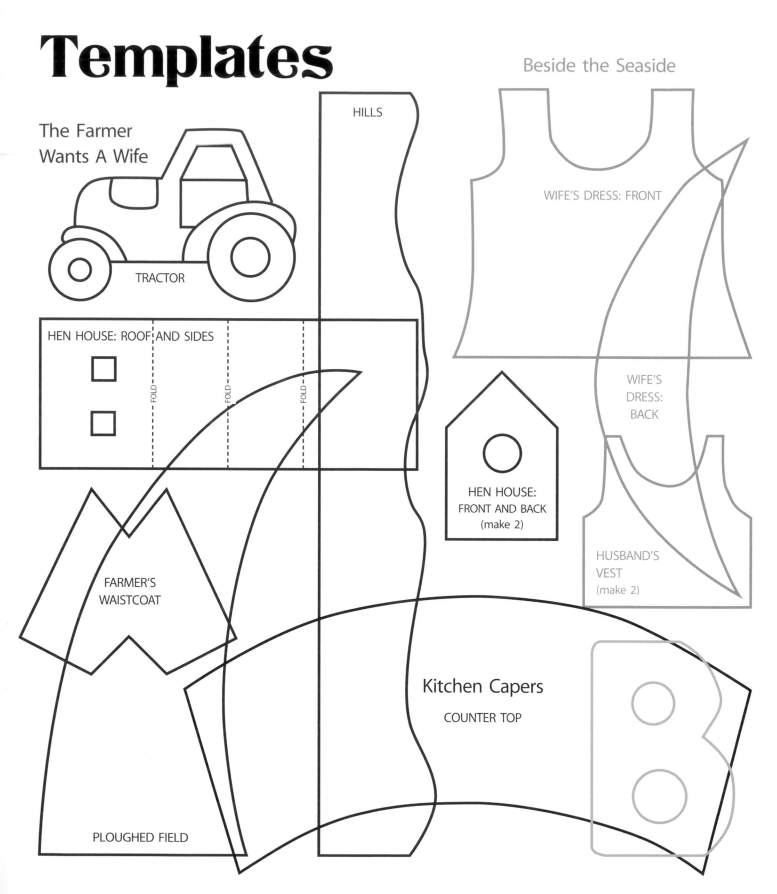

TRACTOR

HILLS

HEN HOUSE: ROOF AND SIDES

FOLD

FOLD

FOLD

WIFE'S DRESS: FRONT

WIFE'S
DRESS:
BACK

HEN HOUSE:
FRONT AND BACK
(make 2)

HUSBAND'S
VEST
(make 2)

FARMER'S
WAISTCOAT

Kitchen Capers

COUNTER TOP

PLOUGHED FIELD

She Caught Her Man

LAPELS (make 2)

CUT

GINGERBREAD
BRIDE AND GROOM
(make 2)

GINGERBREAD
PEOPLE
(make 7)

GROOM'S TAILCOAT

CUT

BRIDE'S DRESS

At the Barre

STAR

Just Bears

LETTERS (enlarge by 141%)

EARS

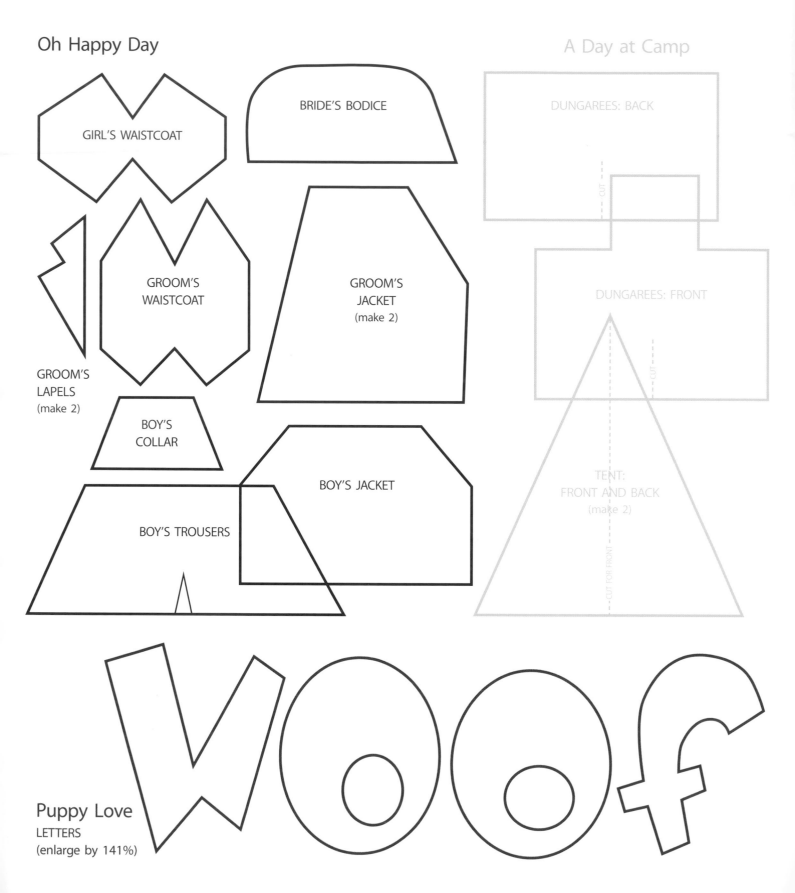

Oh Happy Day

GIRL'S WAISTCOAT

BRIDE'S BODICE

GROOM'S
WAISTCOAT

GROOM'S
JACKET
(make 2)

GROOM'S
LAPELS
(make 2)

BOY'S
COLLAR

BOY'S JACKET

BOY'S TROUSERS

A Day at Camp

DUNGAREES: BACK

CUT

DUNGAREES: FRONT

CUT

TENT:
FRONT AND BACK
(make 2)

CUT FOR FRONT

Puppy Love
LETTERS
(enlarge by 141%)

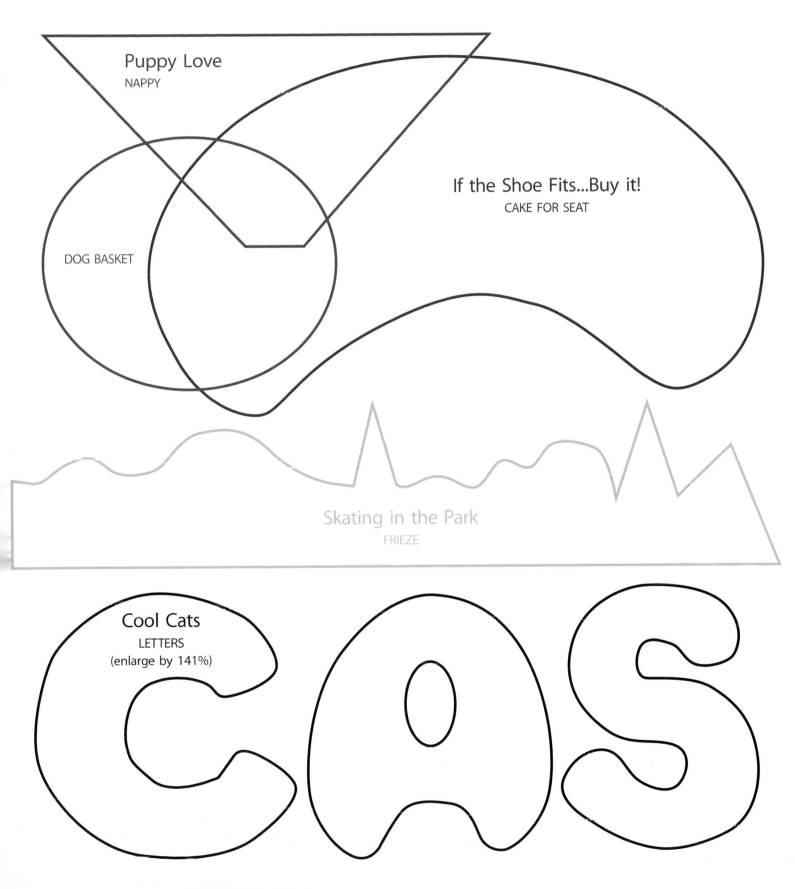

Puppy Love
NAPPY

If the Shoe Fits...Buy it!
CAKE FOR SEAT

DOG BASKET

Skating in the Park
FRIEZE

Cool Cats
LETTERS
(enlarge by 141%)

Gallery

This is some of Maisie's work which has been featured as projects in Cakes & Sugarcraft and Wedding Cakes – A Design Source magazines (published by SKMP).

A Birthday Surprise
(Cakes & Sugarcraft, Issue 89)

Puppy Love
(Cakes & Sugarcraft, Issue 79)

Ribbons and Pearls
(Cakes & Sugarcraft, Issue 84)

Our Hero
(Cakes & Sugarcraft, Issue 72)

Game, Set and Match
(Cakes & Sugarcraft, Issue 81)

Full Steam Ahead!
(Cakes & Sugarcraft, Issues 91-92)

Peep 'n' Sheep
(Cakes & Sugarcraft, Issue 77)

Santa's Christmas Pudding
(Cakes & Sugarcraft, Issue 86)

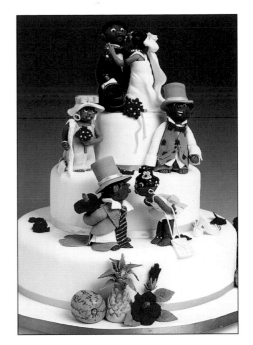

A Caribbean Celebration
(Wedding Cakes – A Design Source,
Issue 8)

The Best Witches
(Cakes & Sugarcraft, Issue 82)

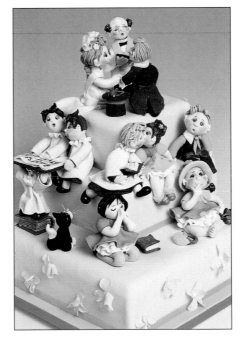

A Marriage Made in Heaven
(Cakes & Sugarcraft, Issue 88)

Happy Birthday
(Cakes & Sugarcraft, Issue 87)

Santa's Little Helper
(Cakes & Sugarcraft, Issue 90)

**Chocolate Heaven
Wedding Cake**
(Cakes & Sugarcraft, Issue 85)

Love is the Key
(Cakes & Sugarcraft, Issue 75)

The Farmhouse Cooker
(Cakes & Sugarcraft, Issue 67)

Happy Holidays
(Cakes & Sugarcraft, Issue 68)

Let's Dance
(Cakes & Sugarcraft, Issue 80)

For a Special Mum
(Cakes & Sugarcraft, Issue 76)

Honky Tonk Piano
(Cakes & Sugarcraft, Issue 83)

The Vicar's Tea Party
(Cakes & Sugarcraft, Issue 89)

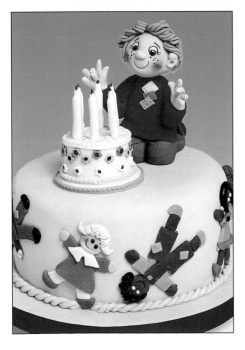

A Birthday Surprise
(Cakes & Sugarcraft, Issue 89)

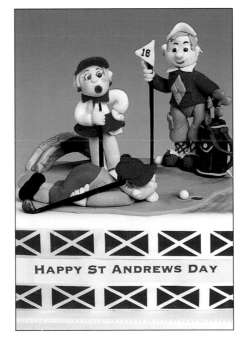

**Tee and Cake on
St. Andrew's Day**
(Cakes & Sugarcraft, Issue 91)

Sheepdog
(Cakes & Sugarcraft, Issue 93)

Stockists

Manufacturers & Distributors

Almond Art
Units 15-16, Faraday Close
Dorse Lane Industrial Estate
Clacton-on-Sea
Essex
CO15 4TR
Tel: 01255 223322
E-mail: sales@almondart.com
Website: www.almondart.com
Mail order and showroom.

CelCakes and CelCrafts (CC)
Springfield House
Gate Helmsley
York
YO41 1NF
Tel: 01759 371447
E-mail: celccrafts@btconnect.com
Website: www.celcrafts.co.uk
Manufacturer of CelSticks, rice and
dot textured rolling pins and bead
makers.

FMM
Unit 5
Kings Park Industrial Estate
Primrose Hill
Kings Langley
Hertfordshire
WD4 8ST
Tel: 01923 268699
E-mail: sales@fmmsugarcraft.com
Website: www.fmmsugarcraft.com
Manufacturers and suppliers of cake
artistry, bakery and catering
equipment.

Guy, Paul & Co. Ltd.
Unit 10, The Business Centre
Corinium Industrial Estate
Raans Road
Amersham
Buckinghamshire
HP6 6FB
Tel: 01494 432121
E-mail: sales@guypaul.co.uk
Website: www.guypaul.co.uk
Trade suppliers of tools and
materials, including Caketime (CT)
and Kemper Tools (KT), for the art of
bakery, sugarcraft and food
decoration.

Holly Products
6 Kings Court
Welsh Row
Nantwich
Cheshire
CW5 5DY
Tel: 01270 625260
E-mail:
enquiries@hollyproducts.co.uk
Website: www.hollyproducts.co.uk
Suppliers of moulds, embossers,
patterns and tools via mail order.

Squires Group
The Grange
Hones Yard
Farnham
Surrey
GU9 8BB
Tel: 0845 61 71 810 (from UK)
+44 (0)1252 260260 (from overseas)
E-mail: info@squires-group.co.uk
Websites: www.squires-group.co.uk
www.cakesandsugarcraft.co.uk
www.squires-exhibition.co.uk

Online shop: www.squires-shop.com
Manufacturer of specialist sugars and
colours, including Sugar Dough;
publishers of Cakes & Sugarcraft
Magazine, Wedding Cakes – A
Design Source and Wedding Dresses
– A Design Source.

Sugar Celebrations
37 Faringdon Road
Swindon
Wiltshire
SN1 5AR
Tel: 01793 513549

80 Westgate Street
Gloucester
GL1 2NZ
Tel: 01793 513549
E-mail: girls@sugarcelebrations.com
Website: www.sugarcelebrations.com

Shops

Jane Asher Party Cakes and Tearoom
22-24 Cale Street
London
SW3 3QU
Tel: 020 7584 6177
E-mail: info@jane-asher.co.uk
Website: www.jane-asher.co.uk
Producer of handcrafted couture
cakes, supplier of baking, decorating
and sugarcraft equipment. Shop,
tearoom and mail order.

Confectionery Supplies
Unit 11 A, B and C
Foley Trading Estate

Hereford
HR1 2SF
Tel: 01432 371451
Shop, school and trade supplier of
Tinkertech Two (TT) products.

Orchard Products (OP)
51 Hallyburton Road
Hove
East Sussex
BN3 7GP
Tel: Freephone 0800 915 8226 /
01273 419418
Website: www.orchardproducts.co.uk
Manufacturers and suppliers of fine
quality sugarcraft cutters and tools.
Shop and mail order.

Squires Kitchen Sugarcraft (SK)
(International School of Cake
Decorating and Sugarcraft)
The Grange
Hones Yard
Farnham
Surrey
GU9 8BB
Tel: 0845 61 71 810 (from UK)
+44 (0)1252 260260 (from overseas)
E-mail: info@squires-group.co.uk
Websites: www.squires-group.co.uk
www.squiresschool.co.uk
Online shop: www.squires-shop.com
Suppliers of sugarcraft colours, tools,
equipment, Sugar Dough,
marzipans and
sugarpastes.
Shop, school
and mail
order.